OUTPATIENT TREATMENT OF ALCOHOLISM

OUTPATIENT TREATMENT OF ALCOHOLISM

A Review and Comparative Study

by

Jeffrey M. Brandsma, Ph.D.
Associate Professor of Psychiatry
University of Kentucky College of Medicine

in collaboration with

Maxie C. Maultsby, Jr., M.D.
Professor of Psychiatry
University of Kentucky College of Medicine
and

Richard J. Welsh, M.S.W.
Associate Professor of Clinical Social Work
University of Kentucky College of Medicine

RC 565
B69
1980

University Park Press
Baltimore

354943

UNIVERSITY PARK PRESS
International Publishers in Science, Medicine, and Education
233 East Redwood Street
Baltimore, Maryland 21202

Typeset by American Graphic Arts Corporation
Manufactured in the United States of America by
The Maple Press Company.

Library of Congress Cataloging in Publication Data
Brandsma, Jeff.
Outpatient treatment of alcoholism.

Bibliography: p.
Includes index.
1. Alcoholism—Treatment.   I. Maultsby, Maxie C.,
joint author.   II. Welsh, Richard J., joint author.
III. Title.
RC565.B69   616.8′61′06   79-9541
ISBN 0-8391-1393-5

CONTENTS

Acknowledgments vii

Introduction 1

chapter 1   **Review of the Literature** 7
chapter 2   **Methodology** 15
chapter 3   **Instrumentation** 39
chapter 4   **Results** 61
chapter 5   **Imported Therapists:**
            A Strategy for Expanding Efficient Alcoholism Services 85
chapter 6   **The Efficacy of Coercion** 95
chapter 7   **Self-Help Methods** 103
chapter 8   **Professional vs. Nonprofessional Treatment** 107
chapter 9   **Summary and Conclusions** 115

Appendices

appendix A
Authorization Form—Voluntary Clients 121
appendix B
Court Referral Form 123
appendix C
Legal Contract Form 125
appendix D
Mental Status Interview 127
appendix E
Drinking Questionnaire and Scoring Key 129
appendix F
Alcoholism Criteria 133
appendix G
**Direction and Rationale for Scoring of the
Modified Gray Oral Reading Test** 137
appendix H
Demographic Questionnaire 141
appendix I
Problem Checklist 149
appendix J
Craving and Withdrawal Questionnaire 151
appendix K
**Behavior Rating Scale and Scoring Keys—Social,
Employment, Economic, and Legal** 157
appendix L
Behavior Rating Scale—Drinking 169
appendix M
Drinking Classification Indices 175

appendix N
Therapist Evaluation Form 185
appendix O
Statistical Tables for Accepted vs. Rejected Clients 189
appendix P
**Dropouts vs. Completors on Screening and
Drinking Questionnaires** 195

References 199
Index 207

ACKNOWLEDGMENTS

The completion of a project with this scope (taking over 7 years) has not been without its problems, conflicts, and successes. Many people were involved directly or cooperatively during the life of this project. In a sense this book is partly theirs, although we take full responsibility for its contents and conclusions.

Dr. Arnold Ludwig, Chairman of the Department of Psychiatry, encouraged us before the grant was written and throughout its history. The National Institute on Alcohol Abuse and Alcoholism (Grant #2RO1 AA0496-05) set up the context of possibility by funding this expensive project. Dr. Kenneth Warren of NIAAA was particularly helpful in seeing us through to completion along with James McDonald from the Research Foundation of the University of Kentucky.

It is fitting to acknowledge in a primary place the project secretaries who did reams of typing, kept things together, handled bureaucratic procedures, dealt with difficult clients, and, indeed, became the foundation of stability and liaison for all our various procedures, persons, and roles. In particular we must thank Sonja Ralston, Beverly Brown, and Edith Shearer for their fine work in these ways as well as a myriad of other things, many of which we were probably not aware of. We are likewise indebted to Gladys Williams for her work on the many drafts that led to a manuscript.

Also, our project social workers made things work with regard to the obtaining of clients, court liaison, follow-up, data collection, and client satisfaction. This was a horrendous, demanding, yet crucial job in many ways. Our appreciation is extended to Margaret Dotson, Murray Oifer, Mary Margaret Brown, and Jane Farmer in this regard.

Mike Cowley served as our lay therapist and also as a part-time data processor after treatment was completed. With regard to his client responsibilities his behavior was exemplary and dedicated. We suspect that many of the good results obtained for his group are in very large part due to his attitude and availability.

Finally, but certainly not in any sense least in importance, are our project directors. Steven Heller was instrumental in getting the project set up and functioning, and Frances Ferguson in carrying it through the middle years. In its final and crucial years we were blessed with three very talented and knowledgeable directors. Their combined knowledge in data gathering and cleaning, computer procedures, and statistics were absolutely essential. Their high standards of scientific rigor kept the authors humble and added greatly to the final results. This book could not have been written without their stellar input. Thus, we acknowledge a great debt to Robert Wetter, Dennis McCarty, and Joseph Fiala, people whom we are sure will make great scientific contribution of their own in the future.

Thus many people, including several unnamed herein, over a very long period of time contributed to this book. Our hope with them is that it will be of some use to those who suffer from alcoholism.

Jeffrey M. Brandsma
Maxie C. Maultsby
Richard J. Welsh

OUTPATIENT TREATMENT OF ALCOHOLISM

INTRODUCTION

Although in recent years much attention has been paid to other drugs of abuse in the media and in national policy, alcohol remains the number one drug of abuse in this country. Alcoholism is a major social and health problem. More than 100 million Americans drink alcoholic beverages, and 6–10 million adults can be classified as problem drinkers, with another 3 million under age 21. Alcoholism affects all levels of society; NIAAA has estimated that 25% of the problem drinkers are white collar, 30% are blue collar, and the largest group (45%) is professional or managerial. Less than 10% of these problem drinkers receive any treatment for their problem.

Alcohol plays an important role in over half of the nation's highway fatalities, in half of its homicides, and in one-third of all suicides. It has been convincingly related to increased cancer and other diseases. The economic cost has been estimated at well over $40 billion annually in lost work time, health and welfare services, and property damage. The human costs ripple throughout the social structure, affecting 45 million others—family, fellow workers, employers, and automobile accident victims. A recent Gallup poll showed almost twice as many respondents reporting alcohol problems in their families than 4 years ago. Despite these costs the per capita consumption in the 1970s is the highest since the 1850s (NIAAA, 1974, 1978). Even in these brief outlines it can be seen that alcoholism is the most serious social and personal dysfunction in the United States, and is worthy of our best efforts in research, treatment, and prevention.

This book is an attempt to explore the possibilities of psychological outpatient treatment for problem drinkers. In 1971, Drs. Jeffrey Brandsma and Maxie Maultsby, and Richard Welsh, M.S.W., found themselves as colleagues in the Department of Psychiatry, University of Kentucky Medical School. Maxie Maultsby was already expert and deeply involved in rational behavior therapy (RBT) applications—particularly self-help maneuvers. Jeffrey Brandsma had just completed his Ph.D. and was interested in the psychotherapies and especially outcome research. In pursuing his career is social work, Richard Welsh had acquired expertise in the community's health care delivery system. It was an amicable marriage of three viewpoints that resulted in a grant request, which was funded by NIAAA in July, 1972, to study various methods in the outpatient treatment of alcoholics.

Our view of alcoholism was loose and catholic. Current theoretical formulations seemed to be in flux, although the public seemed to have, by and large, accepted the disease concept because of the historical traditions and public relations success of Alcoholic Anonymous in the past 30 years (cf. Keller, 1976; Shaw et al.,1978), and because the common physiological reactions to alcoholic overconsumption are widely known (cirrhosis, chronic brain syndrome, and delirium tremors). In contrast, psychoanalytic formulations have emphasized that drinking is a symptom of a more basic personality disorder and that the dependency exhibited in alcoholism is psychological, not chemical. Beyond these influences, in the past two decades learning theorists have provided alternative explanations for heavy drinking, which lead to situational constraints and selective reinforcement treatment programs. Biological and sociocultural theorists and researchers also continue to offer plausible ideas and, less frequently, data to bolster their assumptions about alcoholism (cf. Armor, Polich, and Stambul, 1978, Chapter 2, for a succinct review of these positions and their experimental literature).

Our choice was not to become embroiled in these conceptual controversies, although our inclinations were strongly toward a social learning position. We viewed the behaviors and manifestations of alcoholism as complex interactions between several physiological, social, and psychological factors producing problems in a given individual. We thought it better to take an empirical approach to see if we could identify some of these factors and relate them to different types of treatment outcome. We decided to use theory to identify variables and explain results, but not take a strong a priori position.

Some would now argue with the assertion that there is an urgent need for new, effective treatments for alcoholism which are relatively short-term, economical, and applicable over broad classes of people (i.e., Emrick, 1974), although this was not the case at the inception of our study. Until recently only a few approaches to alcoholism treatment had been tested empirically. The public belief was (and probably is) that Alcoholics Anonymous (AA) was the most effective treatment modality, but no systematic, prospective evaluation of its effectiveness had been undertaken. We decided to apply for a grant to attempt a prospective, comparative study to include an Alcoholics Anonymous group and traditional Insight Therapy as well as a no-treatment control. Two other treatments utilizing the theory and techniques of rational behavior therapy (RBT) were likewise to be compared—professionally delivered RBT to compare with insight therapy and a self-help RBT approach to compare with AA.

The history of the Self Help Alcoholism Research Project (SHARP) from its early inception in July, 1972, was filled with many unique and challenging experiences for the investigators, who considered themselves rather naïve and inexperienced in the ways of grant completion. After recovering from the initial shock of actually being funded, our first official task was to begin interviewing and eventually hiring a competent research director and support staff consisting of a professionally trained social worker and secretary. Advertising, reviewing applications, interviewing candidates, checking references, and negotiating salaries quickly consumed several weeks of valuable project time.

Upon the completion of hiring staff, the major effect was then directed to locating and obtaining an appropriate facility to carry out the actual research. After laboriously looking for office space, we eventually rented a large, two-story, University-owned house conveniently located near our offices at the Medical Center. Massive renovation was first needed to accommodate offices, research space, interviewing rooms, and testing facilities. Shortly after moving in and getting settled, we were unexpectedly informed that our building was scheduled to be torn down and the land was to be used for Medical Center parking. Our plans for community education, development of a referral system, and acquiring patients were of necessity postponed. Instead, all effort was redirected to locating a new facility to rent that would be within our budget, possessed sufficient office space, and was geographically convenient for staff and subjects. New office space was soon acquired that had all the advantages of a centralized urban location near project referral sources and easy accessibility by public transportation. It was essential to have a convenient facility because most testing procedures would be done at this office along with the delivery of psychotherapy by project-employed therapists.

The education of potential community resources and referral agencies regarding the SHARP was the next item of business for the staff. Since SHARP was new and was not the only alcoholic program in the community, its uniqueness, potential contribution, and purpose required careful community integration and understanding. Some agencies quickly perceived SHARP as a "cure all" for all alcohol-related problems; others became immediately competitive, defensive, and even fearful of its potential impact on the service delivery system. Still other agencies expressed ethical concerns, e.g., that SHARP was merely a research project "experimenting on clients" and only offered limited treatment (30 sessions) or even no treatment at all (namely, for those individuals who would be randomly assigned to a no-treatment control group). Last, some self-appointed community caretakers objected strongly to subjects' potential exposure to alcohol as one of our experimental manipulations. These unresolvable dilemmas of clinical research and constraints on treatment persisted in the minds of a limited number of people for the duration of the grant. Despite these difficulties, however, SHARP persevered and did eventually play a significant role in treatment, community education, and research as evidenced through our sponsorship of several alcohol-related workshops ("EMERGENCY TREATMENT") for counselors from all related agencies, participation on numerous multimedia programs, and coordination of a new county-wide referral treatment program for problem drinkers.

By July, 1973, SHARP was ready to select subjects for treatment. Subjects were referred from the local country court system. An effective liason and referral system between the court and the project was developed by our social workers. Basically, the social workers attended all alcohol-related court sessions on a daily basis. They reviewed each court docket, and communicated directly to the presiding judge which individuals seemed appropriate for our research. These individuals were then screened, and, if accepted, were referred to SHARP for treatment.

Additional referrals were actively sought from local industry. One hundred letters were written to industries employing 50 employees or more. Ten companies that manufactured various sizes and types of products were contacted. After initial interest they proved to be reluctant to set up a referral system. Besides denial of problems their reasons for resistance seemed to be:

1. Alcohol problems were of low priority compared to others (for example, strikes). "Fire fighting" was more important.
2. They feared problems with unions if any coercion was used. Other complications were feared.
3. Most managers or foremen did not see alcoholism as having a direct relationship to productivity even though SHARP personnel had carefully researched alcohol-related and Monday morning absenteeism.

Thus we abandoned our industry program and turned to other court systems. As a last resort to acquire additional subjects, SHARP expanded its referral base to include the surrounding county court systems. We did accept self-referred subjects, but these individuals comprised a smaller proportion of our final sample.

While acquiring community acceptance and establishing an adequate referral system, The SHARP eagerly began the task of testing and assigning individuals for treatment. However, our enthusiasm was short-lived due to the city-county merger and subsequent reorganization process, which lasted approximately 4 months. During this time all courts were closed, and referrals were almost nonexistent. This unanticipated delay was coupled with the task of reeducating newly appointed judges and reestablishing the court referral system.

The actual day-to-day business of SHARP was conducted in a suite of offices consisting of three interviewing offices, two large group rooms, and a waiting room, where the secretary was located. On a biweekly basis, the project staff met with three investigators to review the progress of the grant and to discuss administrative issues. The agenda of these administrative meetings typically coincided with the different phases of the grant: establishment of referrals, subject selection, evaluation, treatment, outcome testing, patient follow-up, and data analysis. The daily routine of SHARP would usually include the numerous informal and unexpected visits made by treatment subjects to the office. Since SHARP was convenient to the downtown area and city bus routes, many subjects and their friends frequently stopped by to chat, drink coffee, or even request help for situational emergencies. A considerable amount of professional time was spent resolving transient situational disputes, arranging transportation for stranded subjects, and hospitalizing acutely ill subjects, many of whom were in alcohol withdrawal. SHARP soon acquired the identity as a "home away from home" for many of our subjects and their friends.

In August, 1974, SHARP had successfully acquired its treatment sample, and therefore referrals from the court system and community agencies were terminated. It was difficult for the community to suddenly accept the idea that a well-established treatment program was no longer accepting referrals. In their minds the notion of evaluative research had long been forgotten. In fact, some community caretakers became angry again at the project for terminating therapy and not providing follow-up care. Others reiterated their feelings that research was an expensive waste of time and contrary to patient needs. Recognizing the community's concern for ongoing alcohol treatment programming, the investigators helped establish an outpatient alcohol treatment program at the University of Kentucky Medical Center, Department of Psychiatry, Outpatient Clinic in response to these community needs. Because of change in location, parking, and medical center area, most old patients did not return and few new referrals were forthcoming.

In the spring of 1975, SHARP finally began to address itself to its own priorities, namely, locating and testing all subjects and designating dates for follow-up testing. Locating the treatment subjects plus those assigned to the no-treatment control group was a monumental and time-consuming task. Since most of our sample was of a transient nature, many subjects had moved several times and left no forwarding address. Complicating matters further was the comprehensiveness of our follow-up study, which required testing at 3-month intervals for 1 year. Consequently, gathering follow-up data consumed nearly 16 months of social work time and effort. Concurrently, staff also began the tedious task of organizing, cleaning, and coding of all collected data. This important process was temporarily interrupted on at least three occasions during the fall of 1975 because of night-time burglaries and break-ins. Changing locks, reviewing all inventory, and talking to numerous police investigators distracted staff from the primary task of follow-up testing and coding data.

By the spring of 1976, most of the follow-up testing was completed. As a result, the two project social workers were encouraged to locate different jobs. We did find it necessary at this time, however, to hire part-time research staff knowledgeable in advanced statistical methods to assist us in the final stages of data analysis. The remaining months were devoted to reviewing data and evaluating the results.

In summary, the evolution of SHARP had been a unique and telling set of experiences. The many and often frustrating problems of subject selection, adequate sample size, community referrals and acceptance, the lack of cooperation in industry, bureaucratic hassles, and, finally, data analyses were major hurdles as we strove toward our goal of sharing these results with the public. It is hoped that our efforts will be of some use to those concerned with bringing the problems of alcoholism under control.

chapter 1
REVIEW OF THE LITERATURE

The main purpose of this book is to summarize in appropriate detail the study that was done on an outpatient basis utilizing four treatments of alcoholism. The following chapters concentrate on methodology, instrumentation, results, and implications. Before proceeding, however, our research contribution must be put in context of two strands of expanding empirical endeavor, i.e., comparative psychotherapy outcome research and outpatient alcoholism treatment studies. Reviewing these studies has been rendered immensely easier by the relatively recent appearance of several excellent reviews and studies, to which the reader is referred: Baekeland, Lundwall, and Kissin (1975), Emrick (1974, 1975), Garfield and Bergin (1978), Gurman and Razin (1977), and Luborsky, Singer, and Luborsky (1975) extensively review hundreds of studies; Armor et al. (1978) and Sloane et al. (1975) have excellent reviews and present new data.

The following commentary is designed to generate a perspective and create a context for the current study. Since this is a selective essay of reviews, the reader is encouraged to read the original reviews and further pursue studies of interest.

In a review of 384 psychologically oriented studies spanning 1952–1973, Emrick (1974, 1975) looked at outcome criteria and treatment results. With regard to outcome criteria he found, not surprisingly, that self-reported drinking behavior was the major criterion in 80% of the studies, followed by (as examples) work (26%), family relations (15%), and outpatient treatment (6%). Drinking related positively with two-thirds of the indices (affective-cognitive symptoms, work, home relations, physical condition, arrests, social situations, and AA attendance), but not all, and five studies showed deterioration in other functioning when drinking stopped. Typical results showed (on the drinking criterion) abstinence rates between 10% and 53% and total improvement between 48% and 84% of the sample treated. In general terms, two-thirds were improved or abstinent.

Emrick (1975) found no evidence that treatment techniques are powerful determinants of long-term outcome. Thus he suggested that instead of spending resources on developing new treatents, therapists should get people involved in therapy of any kind, since all treatment techniques seem to have similar degrees of potency. He found that minimal treatment—less than five outpatient sessions or 2 weeks on an inpatient unit—was similar to no treatment, with only 43% just somewhat improved. Treatment produced no difference in abstinence rates compared with no or minimal treatment, but the overall improvement percentages were significantly better when treatment was continued beyond a minimal amount.

In the Luborsky et al. (1975) review, a sophisticated attempt was made to rate the quality of the research and weed out the worst studies. Controlled studies with real, adult, usually nonpsychotic clients were examined; most had been done in the last two decades. (The studies were rated by the same 12 criteria that we had attempted to address at the outset of our study. The constraints of reality and human error make our study criticizable by some of these criteria; as with any human undertaking, the ideal is seldom reached. However, it was not because we were not aware of these criteria or because we did not strive to design a well-conceived and controlled study.) Some major points revelant to the Luborsky review include:

1. Using 13 studies, group psychotherapy was not found to be significantly different overall when compared to individual therapy. This was generally encouraging to us because we had attempted to match experiences across treatment groups on this variable, but did not succeed in any rigorous sense. Their conclusion indicates that these differences in our treatment groups would probably not detract from the overall results.

2. Time-limited therapy produced no different results overall than the time-unlimited therapy. In our study we had to place limits on minimum and maximum participation (attendance) in order to give verbal therapy a chance and yet not let it be interminable. In only a few cases did our 30-session maximum limit the treatment; the majority of our patients did not take advantage of the amount of therapy they could have had. Thus the number of therapy sessions our patients attended and the outcome did not seem to be greatly affected by the imposition of a maximum time or session limit.

3. Of 11 studies comparing results of different schools of treatment (i.e., client centered, psychoanalytic, and Adlerian), only 4 found a significant difference between one school's treatment and another. However, except for five studies of client-centered psychotherapy, there are not enough comparative studies in any one category to draw conclusions about a specific school of treatment. Furthermore, some studies were not acceptably controlled (and not included among the 11); for example, Ellis (1957), with only one therapist (himself) practicing two different treatments, reported that rational-emotive therapy yielded better results than psychoanalytically oriented therapy. The comparisons of client-centered therapy with other psychotherapies disclosed a similar phenomenon—most (four out of five) showed "ties," regardless of what other school it was compared with (i.e., psychoanalytic, neo-Freudian, or Adlerian).

4. Behavior therapy (usually desensitization) was better in 6 of 19 controlled comparisons—usually in brief, low sophistication studies looking

at circumscribed symptoms. It was no different from other forms of psychotherapy in 13 of the 19 comparisons, with more complex symptom patterns employing more general change measures over a longer time period. The overall conclusion was that it is as good as but not necessarily better than traditional therapy.

5. In studies comparing a group treated by psychotherapy with a control group, 20 studies favored psychotherapy, 13 showed no differences.

Some general conclusions drawn by Luborsky et al. (1975) were that except for client-centered and behavior therapy, there has not been enough research to compare schools of psychotherapy. Where comparisons have been made between types of therapy, most studies have found no difference in the proportions of who improves at outcome, but compared to no-treatment controls, psychotherapy of any type seems to yield appreciable gains by and large. The conclusions of the other authors mentioned at the beginning of this chapter are similar.

Three reasons for the lack of differences between types of therapy were suggested:

1. All forms of therapy achieve a moderate to high percentage of improvement so that it becomes hard to differentiate between them statistically.
2. All forms of therapy offer the patient an explanatory guidance system (philosophy) for his behavior.
3. All forms of therapy have potent variables in common, e.g., relationship, suggestion, and clarification (Luborsky et al., 1975).

In their extensive review, Baekeland et al. (1975) only summarized studies that used control groups and statistical analyses. To some this would seem too stringent, especially if the purpose was to be exploratory and searching for new, more effective techniques. However, a strong caveat is provided by Viamontes (1972), who showed that in 89 studies of drug treatment with alcoholic patients, 95% of the uncontrolled studies reported positive results. However, only 6% reported positive results when control groups were utilized. This phenomenon, although perhaps not as extreme, has been documented in other areas of psychiatric research as well.

In this book we look at the overall findings as they relate to outpatient studies wherein drugs were not used. It is the conclusion of Baekeland et al. that evidence does not support the idea that prolonged inpatient treatment offers anything over and above outpatient treatment for randomly selected patients. However, it still seems probable that with appropriate criteria for selection, some patients would benefit more from an inpatient experience.

The area of alcoholism research is deficient generally by its exclusion of lower socioeconomic status (SES) persons and the oppressed majority, women. Dropouts are a key problem. In noncompulsory outpatient treatment, 19%–75% of outpatients dropped out by the fourth session. Chafetz and Blane (1963) found that only 5% of lower SES patients referred to treatment from a hospital emergency room came to treatment. However, they were able to increase this to 65% when a social worker was used to work out the arrangements. In other studies, writing letters, telephoning, putting patients in groups, and seeing families seemed to mitigate against the patient dropping out.

There are many factors associated with the problem of dropping out, but the patient controls most of the variance. Studies have produced a picture of the patient most likely to drop out: socially unstable and isolated, lower SES, symptomatic, dependent yet denying it, ambivalent about treatment, and with some psychopathic features. Since most of our patients were taken from a court system referral, this description applies to the vast majority of our sample. Thus how we handled the problem of dropouts was a key aspect of our study.

Beyond the problems created for research analysis, the problem of dropouts has a morbid and significant aspect to it: these people seem to continue their downward slide socially, physically, and personally. Baekeland et al. (1975) considered them treatment failures. These authors also suggested that most reports of effectiveness could be reduced by one-third if they had taken into account dropouts and deaths.

Once clients have been "hooked" into treatment, the problem arises of which criteria to use to evaluate outcome. Early in the history of alcohol studies the criterion of abstinence was used, if not solely, in a most focal manner. Many arguments have evolved against this practice as sophistication has increased: 1) Patient denial makes this a less reliable measure than occupational stability or legal troubles. 2) Patients improve in some areas of functioning but not in others as a result of treatment. 3) Abstinence is not necessarily related to other areas of life improvement. Indeed, in some studies abstinent persons deteriorate on other criteria. However, in others there are positive correlations to work adjustment, health, and interpersonal and social status. 4) Despite mythology to the contrary (i.e., loss of control theory, "once an alcoholic, always an alcoholic"), some alcoholics can become normal drinkers (3%–50% in various studies, with 15% being an average). 5) Drinking status has been shown to be highly variable in longitudinal studies when individuals are studied. Thus the most reasonable conclusion from both psychotherapy and alcoholism research is that multifactorial outcome measures should be employed without an overdependence on any single one (cf. Foster, Horn, and Wanberg, 1972). This makes eminent sense in that a priori it would seem likely that different therapeutic interventions would have different effects, and different types of alcohol problems would respond differently to treatment(s).

The mean improvement reported by 18 outpatient clinics was 42%, with a standard deviation of 15% (Baekeland et al., 1975). Baekeland et al. suggested that this be tempered and reduced by 5% per year for "spontaneous" improvement. The single most important variable in treatment outcome seemed to be SES. The longer the treatment, the more likely was abstinence, but not necessarily other measures of improvement. In a comparative study of two different types of outpatient therapy with over 700 subjects, Bruun (1963) contrasted 10 individual sessions with a psychiatrist giving medical treatment against a multidisciplinary team approach (i.e., averaging 3 sessions with an internist, 7 with a social worker, 2 in a group, and 20 with a nurse). The two clinics were equivalent in success except that the team approach seemed to be more effective when extraneous influences were partialed out (although obviously they were not equated on the number of sessions). Hayman (1956) found that psychoanalytically inclined psychiatrists were successful with only 10% of their higher SES alcoholics. In highly selected cases, there is some evidence (Gallant et al., 1970) that couple treatment can be effective.

This brief summary shows that very little has been done in evaluating the value of different treatments. This is one of the major contributions of our study.

Baekeland et al. (1975) wrestled with the available data to determine the optional length and types of follow-up. They concluded that a 1-year follow-up seems to be reasonably safe and indicative of the long-term effects of treatment. They suggested that interviews are better than calls, letters, or questionnaires. Whether information given by alcoholics or their relatives is valid and reliable was still moot. They suggested that a 2% per year "spontaneous recovery" rate be subtracted from any follow-up figures.

There are two other issues addressed by our study that need to be mentioned to put them into perspective: compulsory treatment and the effects of Alcoholics Anonymous (AA). Compulsory treatment would seem to be useful with lower SES repeaters and has been shown to be so in early studies (Esterly, 1971; Maier and Fox, 1958). More recently, Gallant et al. (1973) reported very poor results with a skid row population. The conclusion seems to be that, again, SES, the selection of patients, and having powerful enough consequences built into a program accounted for the difference in these results.

In the late 1950s a recognized expert in the field of alcoholism (Fox, 1957) wrote that AA was "probably the single most effective method of treatment." This myth has continued in American society despite a pitifully small data base. More is said on this later, but for introductory purposes a few summary statements of the available data will suffice. "In summary, it seems that the new AA affiliate is most likely to be a single, Class 2–4 individual who has lost his drinking friends and has a supportive wife or girl friend. He is not highly symptomatic, and is a socially dependent, guilt-prone person with obsessive-compulsive and authoritarian personality features, prone to use rationalization and reaction formation" (Baekeland et al., 1975). This is indicative that AA is highly self-selective, does not reach lower class individuals, and probably represents a different population than the one that tends to seek help in a clinic setting.

With regard to outcome in writings that are obviously criticizable, Gellman (1964) estimated that 75% of AA attenders are cured. AA itself (1972) suggests that 60% achieve sobriety within 1 year. Bill C. (1965) reported that 393 persons who attended 10 or more meetings had an improvement rate of 35%—almost the same as for persons attending alcohol specialty clinics. Yet few studies have determined AA's total dropout rate, who drops out, or the long-term effects. Ludwig, Levine, and Stark (1970) presented some retrospective data over a 12-month follow-up after various therapeutic interventions (inpatient) upon alcoholic patients. They found that only 50% of their sample took advantage of AA for the first 3 months, and thereafter followed a steady decline in attendance. At anytime during the follow-up only 20%–30% of their sample was regular attenders; the majority were at best irregular attenders. Likewise there seems to be no relationship to sobriety: 50% of the sober patients did not attend AA and 66% of those who did drank sporadically. Baekeland et al. (1975) pointed out that this rate of improvement is less impressive when considering that this is a self-selected population (i.e., several types of prognostically poor alcoholics—low SES, anti-religious, unaffiliative, and high denial personality traits), and would not end up in a sample that attended 10 sessions or more. Therefore it was concluded that AA probably does a poorer job than most clinics, which offer a wider range of services and thus are applicable to a wider range of patients. AA may be useful as an adjunct or supplemental treatment, but there are few good data available on this. Our current study is one of the few to take a prospective, empirical approach to AA (cf. Emrick, Lassen, and Edwards, 1977; Jindra and Forslund, 1978).

Sloane et al. (1975) provided an excellent discussion of outcome research in psychotherapy, both literature and issues, and their study is a model of sound and thorough research. Basically they found no notable superiority for either broad spectrum behavior therapy or insight-oriented psychotherapy with real outpatients and highly experienced therapists using different techniques, although both therapy groups were better than an untreated control group.

The now notorious "Rand Report" (Armor et al., 1978) has received much negative publicity concerning its assertions on the possibility of controlled drinking. Their data and methodology are as good as any available in the field of alcohol research—which is not to assert much. We do not wish to enter the lists of healthy controversy (cf. Emrick and Stilson, 1977), but rather to point out that Armor et al.'s review of alcoholism conceptual models and treatments (Chapter 2) is incisive and succinct, and should be read (along with their study) to inform oneself of the field and important issues. Later our results are related to these studies when they are comparable.

This book compares four specifically defined types of psychotherapy and a no-treatment control group for randomly assigned alcoholics on a wide range of outcome variables and for a 1-year follow-up. Other issues, such as compulsory treatment and "imported therapists," are also addressed in an empirical fashion. How this was accomplished is the subject of the following two chapters.

chapter 2
METHODOLOGY

This study summarizes the results of 5 years of investigation into the problems of outpatient treatment with alcoholics. It was designed to examine the efficacy of four treatment modalities in terms of several variables at outcome and during a 1-year follow-up.

This chapter presents the design of the study and explains in necessary detail the rationale for our procedures. The next chapter deals with the dependent measures and their rationale. It is only in the context of these operational procedures and sample characteristics that our results can be fully understood and appropriately generalized.

The starting point for these considerations must be the context. Lexington, Kentucky, is a moderate-size city of slightly over 200,000 people that has been a rapidly growing urban center over the last decade. During the tenure of our study the city and county governments merged in order to form a more representative government and provide more efficient services. Surrounding Lexington are smaller, more rural communities, such as Paris and Winchester. Our social workers worked out agreements with the court and parole systems of these towns for referral of alcoholic patients to our project.

SHARP was housed in a suite of offices near the University of Kentucky. Its location was on a major traffic artery only 3 blocks from the downtown area. Full-time employees of most import were the secretary (bureaucracy expert, receptionist, assistant social worker, and jack-of-all-trades) and the two project social workers. For its first 4 years the project had a full-time research director and some part-time clerks. At its finish we employed graduate students as research associates and undergraduates as coders.

THERAPISTS

Psychotherapy outcome studies have been often criticized because they use inexperienced graduate students or professionals-in-training as their therapists. This criticism is thought to be especially appropriate to any study trying to test a dynamic or psychoanalytic approach, which requires years of training and experience to conduct properly. We attempted to get highly experienced therapists for the two professional groups in our study in an attempt to give these treatments maximum possibility of having impact.

Insight Therapy

The insight therapy was conducted by six professionals—three Ph.D.s, one Ed.D., one M.D. (Board Certified in Psychiatry), and one M.S.W. Their years of experience at the end of the project ranged from 5 to 23, with a mean of 14 years. All of these had had some continued training in the form of workshops (e.g., family therapy, Gestalt therapy, behavior modification, transactional analysis).

This was an experienced group, and there is some evidence that experienced therapists in the insight orbit tend to make similar kinds of interventions (Fiedler, 1950). However, there also exists the possibility that, as one's experience increases, so too does individuation of style and approach. We did not attempt the impossible task of changing anyone's basic style or language, but rather attempted to have them all share common conceptions of the dynamics of alcoholism. If this could be accomplished, the verbal interventions of therapy would be expected to be more homogeneous in this group. To this end we had Dr. Louis Cancellaro provide a 2-day workshop on the dynamics of alcohol dependence from a psychodynamic viewpoint. How much impact this had on attenuating differences and providing a homogeneous treatment is difficult to assess, but it in itself would probably have to be evaluated as minimal. Nevertheless, the attempt was made and was expected to build on a common assumptive core present in these men. A later study (reported in the results chapter) showed the insight type of therapy to be discriminably different from RBT.

RBT—Professional

The RBT professional group was made up of one Ph.D., one M.D. (Board Certified in Psychiatry), three M.S.s, and two M.S.W.s. Their years of experience as of the end of the project ranged from 3 to 17 years, with a mean of 8 years. All but two had had post-degree training, such as various workshops, and one had returned to graduate school to work on a Ph.D. More important, all had received training from Dr. Maultsby in RBT and thus had a consistent approach to follow. One other M.S. psychologist with 2 years of experience in RBT functioned as a group therapist during the final phases of treatment. After the patients had received some individual sessions they were encouraged to attend this group concurrently. As it turned out this person conducted approximately 15 group sessions over a 4-month period, with an attendance of usually two to four men—usually the same ones. All of the authors were therapists in this group.

RBT—Nonprofessional

The RBT lay patients turned out usually to receive individual therapy because of scheduling problems. This treatment was administered by an ex-drug abuser who was working on his bachelor's degree in psychology (which he acquired near the end of the project). He had had no experience except having been treated by and thus learned RBT in helping himself. Beyond this he had attended a 2-day workshop taught by Drs. Albert Ellis and

Maultsby. Thus this treatment was administered by one person who used the same theory and techniques as the professional RBT therapists.

Alcoholics Anonymous

An AA treatment group was started at SHARP by contacting the local AA organization. They sent two volunteers, a man (with a B.S.) and a woman (with a high school education), to begin our new group. They had 14 and 10 years of experience in AA, respectively. The AA group was open to all who would attend and was conducted by one or the other of these people for approximately 1 year until January, 1973. By that time (the beginning of the research in terms of assigning patients), a member of the group (not included in the research project) had become very adept at running meetings. This minority group member, who had a 9th grade education, had had no AA experience before modeling himself after the two initial leaders of this group. This person remained the leader for the rest of the time of the research project (with a 3-week hiatus when an experienced AA counselor filled in), and continues to be involved in AA today. He received no remuneration for this, but was very cooperative in providing attendance reports to the project.

Payment

Professional therapists were paid $25.00 per session. For each client they accepted, they were paid $10.00 for each missed appointment up to three times per patient, or a total of $30.00. After that they were not reimbursed for scheduled appointments wherein the client did not show up. The RBT lay therapist was paid initially at a rate of $15.00 per group or individual session. As his involvement in therapy terminated he was kept on for other work on an hourly rate. The RBT group therapist was also paid $15.00 per session.

From the inception of the project we planned to pay our subjects after treatment was completed as an incentive to their cooperation in obtaining follow-up data. Soon after the project began, however, we noticed a great loss of subjects between court referral, initial testing, and attendance at the first therapy session (Brandsma et al., 1977). Thus early on we instituted the procedure of promising a man $10.00 for his time used to complete the testing battery (3–4 hours). However, this money was not paid until the man had attended his first therapy session. No data were kept on the effectiveness of this procedure, but our definite impression was that this incentive was very effective in reducing our previously high dropout rate.

Each subject was informed that he would be paid $15.00 for completing the outcome battery and for each follow-up session that he attended. If data on outcome and all four follow-up interviews were obtained, the man would be given a bonus of $20.00.

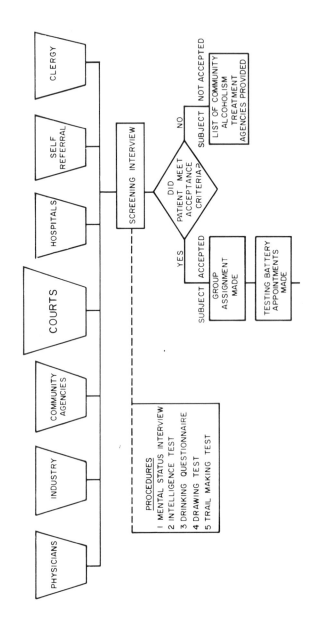

PHYSICIANS · INDUSTRY · COMMUNITY AGENCIES · COURTS · HOSPITALS · SELF REFERRAL · CLERGY

SCREENING INTERVIEW

PROCEDURES
1 MENTAL STATUS INTERVIEW
2 INTELLIGENCE TEST
3 DRINKING QUESTIONNAIRE
4 DRAWING TEST
5 TRAIL MAKING TEST

DID PATIENT MEET ACCEPTANCE CRITERIA?

NO — SUBJECT NOT ACCEPTED — LIST OF COMMUNITY ALCOHOLISM TREATMENT AGENCIES PROVIDED

YES — SUBJECT ACCEPTED — GROUP ASSIGNMENT MADE — TESTING BATTERY APPOINTMENTS MADE

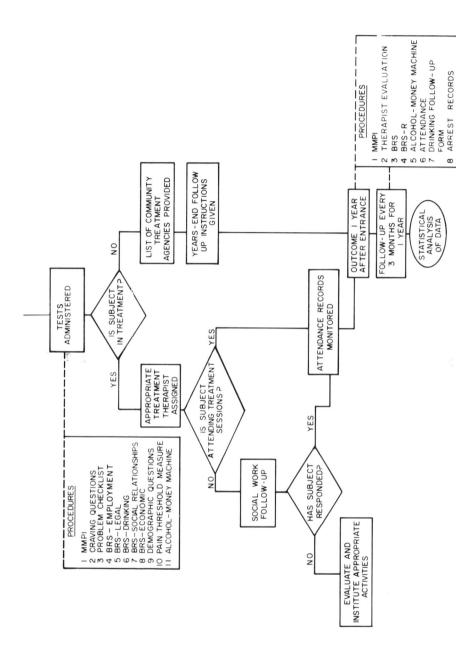

Figure 1.   SHARP patient flow chart and dependent variables.

Figure 1 is a graphic representation of the flow of patients through the SHARP treatment process. It provides an overview of the procedures and where they intervened in time. Figure 1 shows that no matter what the source of referral, all potential subjects were required to pass through a screening procedure. This procedure was employed in order to define our sample more accurately. Individuals who came for treatment may not, in fact, have had "alcoholism," or when sufficient alcohol-related problems were present, those may have been confounded by psychiatric or neurological problems. Therefore, to eliminate individuals from the study who did not appear to be alcoholic and/or who had severe psychiatric, neurological, or intellectual deficits, which the project was not designed to treat, the screening procedures were instituted.

SCREENING PROCEDURES

Originally we planned only to take men between the ages of 30 and 50 years. This remained our ideal, but as the project progressed our limits expanded to the available subjects, with the range being between 24 and 58 years. The screening consisted of the administration of the following procedures, in this order:

1.   Mental Status Interview (see Appendix D)
2.   Intelligence Test
3.   Drinking Questionnaire (see Appendix E)
4.   Drawing Test
5.   Trail Making Test
6.   Reading Test

These tests are reviewed specifically in the next chapter.

Many of our Ss were screened immediately following their appearance before the judge unless they were still intoxicated. If they were intoxicated, 24–48 hours or longer would be allowed to elapse before their testing. When they were screened would depend on the social worker's judgment of their being intoxicated. We are aware that it can often take 7 to 10 days for a person to detoxify; thus, some of our Ss probably were still under the influence of alcohol. However, this would tend to introduce a conservative bias, i.e., excluding them from the sample. Many were given an appointment at our offices to come in for screening within a few days. A social worker trained in interviewing and the use of these instruments would conduct the interview. On certain questions the interviewer would probe for complete responses. The performance tests would be administered as closely as possible according to the directions given in the manuals for these tests. The total time was usually less than 1 hour.

Over the 5 years of this project there were inconsistencies across various interviewers in their administration and in their judgment of whether a man was intoxicated. However, the relative objectivity of our procedures and the relative integrity of our social workers leads us to believe that in sum these mistakes were not substantial, and that the decisions and results made from these procedures were valid overall. The procedures and their scoring are discussed in the next chapter ("Instrumentation") more specifically. A discussion of the decision rules employed are stated here:

> Any *conclusive* signs of bizarre thinking can be considered as reason for eliminating a client's candidacy for our program. If a client's thinking and ideations appear appropriate, then two clear failures on the subsequent tests constitute unacceptance for further consideration.
>
> One clear failure on the tests and borderline scores on the other tests may be mitigated against by a client's meeting at least two of the four following criteria:
>
> 1. Living with significant other
> 2. Gainful employment
> 3. Continuous residency in the community
> 4. Being desirous and self-motivated to seek help with his drinking problem and so indicating
>
> If there are no clear failures, but the client is otherwise borderline, then one of the four above criteria must additionally be met for positive consideration. Criterion number one is the most significant, number four the least significant.

Obviously there is room for judgment and thus human error in this procedure. However, judgment was confined to cases that were by empirical procedures and scoring defined as borderline. We believe that this mix of empiricism and judgment is a good one, and one that allowed us to achieve our ends, i.e., the collection of a well-defined sample of individuals having problems with alcohol.

If a subject was excluded from the sample, he was given a list of alcoholism-related services provided by various community agencies and a modicum of encouragement and help in contacting an appropriate agency. Those accepted were informed immediately of the scope and expectations of the project, how much money they could earn by complying, and the consequences of dropping out. More specifically they were told that the treatment was free, was in lieu of a jail sentence, and would last up to a year with a year follow-up. They could earn up to $85.00 if they completed follow-up. If they did not continue treatment for an agreed-upon time up to 1 year, the court would be informed and the judge could reimpose a 30-day jail sentence. Our project social worker would act as these persons' parole agent. Specific forms of authorization, referral, and contract are reproduced in Appendices A, B, and C. Each voluntary client would sign only the authorization form for voluntary clients (see Appendix A). Initially the court-referred clients signed a form similar to Appendix A. However, shortly after its inception the project switched to the more binding form found in Appendix C for court-referred clients only. It should be at least briefly mentioned here that the evolution of these forms and a working relationship with the courts took a lot of time and effort, and the people involved from both ends deserve our appreciation. Initially judges were reluctant to refer to our project. We questioned them on their reasons and obtained the following:

1. Newness of our resource—lack of knowledge of such
2. Lack of established system of referral
3. Competition of other agencies for patients, i.e., Community Mental Health, various alcoholism programs
4. Paperwork involved
5. Unsure of legal grounds in sending men to our project rather than sentencing
6. Certain previous employees of project had "turned them off"

It is a credit to our project staff that these problems were worked through favorably over time, and that a good, working relationship was obtained. More is said of the effects of this relationship in Chapter 6.

Many patients were screened at court and then referred to our offices; others were referred and then screened at the office. When they arrived and were acceptable, they were tested immediately if there was time. If not, they were scheduled as soon as possible (usually within 48 hours). After passing the screening test and having their name reported to the project secretary, the patients would be randomly assigned to one of five groups. This was accomplished by assigning a number to each of the groups in the following manner:

1. Rational behavior therapy—professional
2. Rational behavior therapy—lay administered
3. Insight therapy
4. Alcoholics Anonymous
5. Control group

Each number was written on a slip of paper and was sealed in envelopes. Equal quantities of each number were used. The envelopes were shuffled extensively and then numbered in order on the outside. As each patient was accepted into the project the next envelope in order was drawn, opened, and the patient was thus assigned randomly to the treatment. While the patients were being tested, the project secretary contacted one of the therapists in the assigned group in order to have an appointment time and name ready for the client upon completion. After having 31 *Ss* assigned to the control group, we stopped this assignment to increase the numbers in the treatment groups.

Very shortly after beginning the project we instituted procedures designed to decrease our early dropout rate. As mentioned, one of these was to pay the men in groups 1–4 $10.00 for completion of the testing battery—but not until after they had attended their first session. Control *Ss* were paid immediately after testing, at which time they were also given a list of all community alcoholism services with names and telephone numbers and were encouraged to make use of whatever seemed appropriate for them. They were informed that they would be contacted in a year to be tested again.

The initial testing battery was a series of empirical instruments designed to assess the project goals as measures of change or predictors of outcome. This total battery would take from 3 to 4 hours, depending on the man. The predictive and outcome measures involved in approximate order of administration follow; description and rationale are included in the next chapter.

Initial Testing Battery

1. Demographic Questionnaire
2. Minnesota Multiphasic Personality Inventory (MMPI)
3. Behavior Rating Scale (BRS)
4. Problem Checklist
5. Craving and Withdrawal Questions
6. Finger Pain Threshold
7. Predictor Paradigm
8. Working for money and alcohol

TREATMENTS—EXPERIMENTAL GROUPS

Insight Therapy

Theory   It is difficult in a chapter on research methodology to attempt to summarize what the treatment called "insight therapy" really is. Certainly there were vast differences in the personal styles of the therapists that administered this treatment. Yet there is a tradition and philosophy, which can be traced back to Freud, that has emphasized insight in the therapeutic situation. Jerome Frank (1973, pp. 207–212), in his wise book *Persuasion and Healing*, has called these psychoanalytic derivatives "evocative" therapies, and describes adequately their assumptions and attitudes toward treatment.

Just what is "insight" in therapy?[1] Certainly it is not all that is involved in therapy, nor does it speak to the proper conditions under which it occurs, i.e., with a certain relationship and preparation. Insight has the sense of a *new, organizing perspective realized abruptly*. It has the quality of a self-acquisition, not something the therapist has been trying to convey. This perspective integrates previously unrelated experiences and thus enhances the sense of power of the self, i.e., as a preexisting state of affairs becomes evident or conscious, it is now subject to criticism, judgment, and control. This capacity is also necessary for the therapist as he attempts to define and direct the therapeutic process.

As a result of this emotive reconceptualization process the patient comes to understand his symptoms in relationship to his experiences, their historical development, and present situation. Symptoms (alcoholism) become secondary to or symbolic of the residues of the person's willful, needful misunderstandings of others, himself, his body, and the world. When these relationships are made clear through insight, as well as gradual understandings, the patient can make better decisions about what to affirm and where he stands in the world—even with regard to his drinking behavior.

Redlich and Freedman (1966) claim two assumptions in the psychoanalytic approach: that unconscious processes exist and that they can be interpreted. Insight involves making unconscious feelings conscious. Psychoanalytically oriented therapy (in contrast to classical psychoanalysis) is more concerned with current personality dynamics and problems and less concerned with a complete reconstruction of one's past life. The patient talks of his thoughts, feelings, and experiences in a permissive atmosphere. This leads to an experiencing and talking about his emotions—anxiety, shame, or guilt. The therapist is accepting, listens carefully, and makes timely interpretations or clarifications. Insight therapy emphasizes mutual *understanding* of *unconscious* dynamics, often by *interpretation*. One content area would be the present relationship between the therapist and the patient, but ideally all insights are encouraged to be applied in one's present life.

As mentioned earlier, our experienced insight therapists participated in a 2-day workshop given by Dr. Louis Cancellaro (previous Associate Director of Lexington's Narcotics Hospital and Research Center) so that they might have a common basis in thinking about their patients. It was stressed conceptually that addiction is symptomatic; dependence on a substance provides pleasure and alleviates psychic pain. There is no such thing as an "alcoholic personality," but certain traits or dynamic mechanisms are found more frequently in those who become addicted. Alcoholism was said to be

---

[1] The authors are indebted to Dr. Erling Eng for the following discussion on the nature of insight.

caused by multiple factors—environmental, physiological, social, and psychological.

Although there have been many attempts to classify alcoholics, a simple dichotomous one was employed as a foundation—the "primary" (essential) and "secondary" (symptomatic) alcoholic. Primary alcoholics are severely characterological, having received insults to their development and severe repression in the oral stage (first year). They have an extremely high need for immediate gratification and are egocentric and narcissistic. Their primary defense mechanisms are denial and projection. They are often seen as borderline characters in depressed and/or paranoid states. Prognosis is extremely guarded.

Secondary alcoholics had their primary personality formation experiences in the anal stage of development (second and third years). These persons are able to recognize others as individuals but are competitive, rebellious, and resistive. They might strive aggressively for mastery at the expense of others. There may be homosexuality and, at times of decompensation, paranoid states.

Beyond this classification based on psychoanalytic developmental theory, two other types of personality structure were discussed with regard to alcoholism. The first was a "phallic-Oedipal type," characterized by ambivalence toward members of the opposite sex and usually involved in a marriage of dependent hostility. A second type was "hysterical," characterized by histrionic and manipulative behavior. Prognosis for both of these types is considerably better than for that of the primary alcoholic.

With this underpinning, alcoholics were discussed in terms of their general dynamics. Six traits were described:

1. Strong tendency to regress under stress.
2. Use of primitive defense mechanisms, such as acting out in aggressive and sexual ways when drunk, but acting very differently and opposite when sober.
3. Massive usage of denial, of which blackout *might* be a form.
4. Marked dependency on environmental supports. The alcoholic has learned how to provoke the environment to act on his behalf.
5. Harsh conscience or superego, which produces much fear and guilt.
6. Narcissistic, egocentric, passive, demanding behaviors—an infantile way of coping. Thus to some extent other individuals are seen only as objects to be manipulated into taking care of one's needs.

Persons with these structures in their personality tend to get caught in vicious cycles of frustration and psychic pain. One way out temporarily is to use a chemical substance to be relatively less miserable. Unfortunately this almost inheritantly leads to self-destructive patterns of coping—more denial, projection, introjection, and more alcohol.

Insight treatment must look beyond the presenting behavior and toward the underlying conflicts or feelings that become salient when the patient is drunk. This is problematic because the person with alcohol problems does not want to increase his psychic tension or frustration; he has a basic ambivalence toward help. However, if he will remain in treatment for 5–10 sessions, his initial resistances can be examined and overcome.

According to Dr. Cancellaro, the behavior of drinking is a problem in itself. It must be stopped and the patient must be in a stabilized living situation if self-exploration is to occur. At this point the therapist could discuss and formulate mutual goals with the client. Everything cannot be accomplished by reflection and talk—goals must be set and behavior change expected. When necessary, limits are to be set on in-therapy behavior and contracts made for extra-therapy behavior change.

One of the primary goals is to create conditions in which the patient can confront and explore himself, and not develop an uproar in the environment. This is difficult because persons with character disorders are adept at externalizing their problems. However, the thrust is to make them more neurotic, i.e., to internalize and encapsulate their problems. Then problems can then be worked on one at a time, and responsible behavior change can begin.

Another major goal is to use various ways to encourage transference so that it can be understood by the patient. Evidence of transference and other manipulations (games) must first be collected and later interpreted at the proper time. With insight and emotive reconceptualization, judgment becomes interposed between one's impulses and one's coping mechanisms. In the case of alcoholics, the coping mechanism is drinking.

Insight therapy, when done correctly, was to emphasize how a person gets things to happen to himself in the present, not how previous experiences taught him to react (although obviously the two are related). There was little emphasis placed on reconstruction of the past. If historical material emerged, the therapists were encouraged to "hook these up" as soon as possible to present situations and problems. Mutual goals were stressed and it was suggested that treatment be partialed into various sectors of the patient's life as the self-exploration proceeded. Only the historical material necessary for each sector or goal was utilized—again, total reconstruction was eschewed.

At various renegotiation points or plateaus in treatment it was suggested that family members be called for consultation to help decide if more exploration was desirable or necessary. Termination ideally occurred when goals had been reached in reality, not when another resistance arose. These goals did not have to include continued abstinence.

Practice   We tried to set up flexible guidelines for our therapists. They could have from one to three sessions per week; three sessions were used if a man was in crisis. Up to four sessions could be used to bring in the family members or spouse. Therapists could combine their patients into groups if they desired. The total amount of therapy sessions, however, was originally set at 40 hours—later this was reduced to 30. As it turned out only a few patients used all the therapy time available to them individually, and almost never did a therapist have a marital, family, or group session. All sessions were taped on cassettes that we provided. At the end of treatment patients were told that they could be seen on an emergency basis for support during the year of follow-up, but sequential sessions were discouraged by the project investigators.

Rational Behavior Therapy (RBT)—Professional

Theory   RBT is a system of treatment based on the cognitive therapy (rational emotive therapy) formulated by Albert Ellis (1962) coupled with learning theory and behavior therapy conceptions. The approach has its roots in the orientation of the early Stoic philosophies and has been clearly elucidated in two recent publications by Goodman and Maultsby (1974) and Maultsby (1975). Its relationship to classical conditioning theory is elucidated by Russell and Brandsma (1974). Specific applications to alcoholism can be found in Maultsby (1979).

RBT is a highly directive method of enabling people to teach themselves how to increase their reasoning and behavioral skills so that they can better understand and cope with the stresses of everyday living. If one can learn to reason logically and rationally, emotions will be under better control and problems will be perceived more clearly, thus allowing a more efficient solution.

Rational thinking or behavior: a) is based on objective facts, not subjective opinions, b) preserves one's life, c) helps an individual achieve personally defined goals, and d) enables a person to function with a minimum of internal and external conflict. In RBT mechanistic conditioning procedures may be employed, but these are controlled by the patient, whose goal is to train himself to think and behave rationally. Thus the patient trains himself in personally desirable cognitive and physical behaviors (emotions will follow) so that he can progressively become independent of others for most of his psychological needs.

RBT is based on some assumptions which, taken together, sharply differentiate it from other therapies. These are:

1. Disorders of the emotions and of overt behavior are the result—not the cause—of irrational thinking. The conventional view of the disturbed person is that his emotions have some hidden, underlying disorder within them that is causing the problem, and, incidentally, is producing cognitive and perceptual disability. RBT reverses this relationship:

cognition is the "lens of the mind," and distortions that it produces create havoc in thinking processes and then in the nervous system and the entire physiological apparatus. It makes sense, therefore, to begin by treating cognition; by making it more rational, emotional relief will result naturally.

2. If consciousness without toxicity is available, then the individual is responsible for his behavior. The individual is responsible in the sense that he is producing his thoughts and his behaviors, and hence he and he alone can change them. Furthermore, RBT holds that it is important to make him feel and accept this responsibility, because it is from a growing sense of responsibility that he begins to learn how to pull his thinking out of the ruts he has allowed himself to fall into. The concept pushes against the disturbed individual's constant tendency to split his personality in order to evade responsibility for change and render himself incapable of change. This concept of single responsibility is not just a gimmick or a Band-Aid; it is an objective fact and an idea implicit in all forms of psychotherapy.

3. A person does not have to upset himself or be disturbed by people and events around him. A person has the ability to insulate his feelings from attempts by other disturbed people in his environment to upset him. RBT goes so far as to challenge the individual thus: Why upset yourself about anything? At first, this idea sounds absurd, not only to patients, but even to apparently normal people who are accustomed to believing that it makes sense to react emotionally to emotional and inappropriate behaviors of others. A corollary to the question about not upsetting oneself about anything is: What purpose would getting upset serve? This introduces the value system of limiting one's mental energies to the kind of thought that is useful and functional in helping the person advance toward his various goals throughout the day, rather than squandering valuable mental energies on self-defeating emotions.

4. A person can literally "think what he wants to think." He can decide to discontinue a train of thought; he can order up a thought and think it; he does not have to think a certain way just because he has always thought that way. Nor does he have to behave the way he has long behaved. It is precisely at the highest cognitive level—where we make the decision about what we want to think and how we therefore want to feel—that we possess the most leverage for emotive and behavioral change. This contradicts the concept implicit in behavior therapy that behavior (even motive behavior) is best changed by associational techniques involving rewards and punishments—techniques that are quite successful in the lower species. Man, however, finds it only too easy to sabotage this association from within, by the simple act of not changing his attitudes and ideas about things.

5. All people are merely fallible human beings. If one could stop using this concept to avoid individual responsibility, it could become an effective, tension-relieving insight preventing neurotic perfectionism. A person can thus become more tolerant of others and himself; he can protect himself from unrealistic "oughts and shoulds" and the anxiety they produce. This understanding has the potential of eliminating a significant source of anxiety that was previously dealt with through the use of alcohol (cf. Brandsma, 1976).

6. Most behavioral and emotional disorders have irrational "thinking" as their common denominator. One disorder does not lead to another; all are the product of the same irrational thinking process that prevails in the cognitive portion of the brain. Thus, a person cannot say he will get over his alcoholism as soon as he learns to stop attacking himself, because he has hidden within his cognition some ideas (most often non sequiturs) about how drinking helps him "feel better" and how he cannot help indulging when he sees alchoholic beverages. These beliefs are just as important in maintaining the drinking/self-attack syndrome and relapse (cf. Marlatt and Gordon, 1979) as are equally irrational ideas about personal worthlesssness. This is an important concept of RBT, because it helps the patient avoid delaying treating himself for one part of the syndrome "until another part is cleared up," a tendency that is commonly a part of the neurotic pattern.

7. It is objectively meaningless to speak of how things "should" have been, because obviously the conditions for their having turned out any other way simply did not exist. Therefore, what is, is, because the conditions for having brought it into existence preceded it.

8. *Dependence*, even on a therapist, is an undesirable state for a person, and he should be put on his own, after a brief but intensive therapeutic period, as early as feasible. When on his own, the patient's progress ideally would be monitored and rechecked. Ideally, in RBT he is able to come and go freely, rather than considered "discharged." The primary job of the rational therapist is to build autonomy, which is typically a missing element in the neurotic structure.

9. The seemingly mysterious "persistence factor" that seems to block or undo so many therapies is not due to "unresolved early childhood conflicts" that must be analyzed and resolved, but to the simple principle of inertia. Viewing the problem in this light removes much of the self-defeating fearfulness from the persistence and reduces it to manageable proportions that can be overcome by rational thinking.

RBT theory rejects the notion that original causation can be known accurately. Therefore, prolonged analysis of past events is unnecessary in a person's attempts to overcome emotional or mental problems. Instead,

RBT focuses primary attention cross-sectionally on the person's present behavior. Changes can only take place in the present.

Very early in RBT the person learns how to reduce the intensity of his undesirable emotions quickly so that the reasoning portion of his brain is free for clearer thinking. That mental maneuver first involves a relentless challenging of emotionalized thoughts in the light of objective reality. Second, the individual learns to replace his old self-defeating, emotionalized thoughts with more rational ones by himself. This is accomplished through the use of mental health-improving homework. This technique of self-analysis teaches the person how to examine in writing the thoughts he has when he is experiencing emotional or mental discomfort; then, sentence by sentence, he challenges each of these thoughts in the light of the rational criteria, correcting or replacing faulty ones.

As his skill in homework increases, the person finds himself performing this self-correcting mental maneuver automatically. Written homework then becomes progressively less necessary as the habit of rational thinking becomes a part of his entire thinking process. As his thinking or reasoning power grows, he finds himself more and more capable of controlling old self-defeating habits of emotional response. At that stage, the person is in the midst of the process of rational self-mastery.

The degree of success with RBT depends on the intensity of its application; the aim is to overcome self-defeating thinking habits of long standing. As with all habits, these tend to persist unless challenged rationally and repeatedly by the individual.

In addition to self-analysis every time he has an emotional or mental disturbance, the person is often asked to tape record his self-disclosure discussions with his rational associates (laymen who have learned the process of rational self-mastery, via reading or personal RBT) or with a mental health professional. The tape provides a permanent record of helpful discussions that can be listened to repeatedly. Such repetition makes the difference between rational and irrational thinking clearer to him. In effect, it conditions his mind to understand and apply this more humanistic way of thinking.

RBT removes the mystery from psychotherapy and gives the patient and the mental health professional the tools to perform the patient's cure in the shortest period of time at the least expense. To accomplish this, RBT theory simplifies therapeutic concepts and procedures so they can be applied effectively as self-therapy. Even though emotionally distressed, a person always possesses some control and can concentrate, intensify, and direct the process of rational self-mastery with as much efficiency as he chooses.

Practice   The modal therapeutic experience in professional RBT consisted of weekly 30–45 minute tape-recorded individual sessions. As with insight therapy, more than one session could be scheduled per week if necessary. Although systematic written homework was encouraged for as many life events as were problematic, the educational level and resistance of many of our clients precluded an extensive use of this technique. Between the sessions the patient was scheduled to listen to his tape of the previous sessions alone. In addition, he could listen to any other of his tapes as often as he liked. Whenever possible these patients were encouraged to view videotapes of Dr. Maultsby discussing alcoholism with a group of inpatients. If they could read, they were also given cartoons[2] exploring the rational view of alcoholism and its treatment. After a number of individual treatment sessions, patients were to be referred to a professionally run group to continue their new learnings in RBT; few availed themselves of this opportunity.

In therapy itself the patients were taught the A-B-C theory of emotions (i.e., perception leads to cognition, which leads to emotion) and the criteria for rational thinking and behavior through discussion of their problems. Then the treatment was individualized in that those who would admit to having internal conflicts would be encouraged to talk about their thinking and complete rational self-analysis (RSA) homework assignments. The many resistive alcoholics who would only admit to having external problems (wife, family, police, drinking) would be persuaded to self-administer a behavioral change program that involved scheduling, stimulus control procedures, sipping, and keeping a log of frequency and amount. Later, if they began talking about their internal problems, techniques would change. Upon their request, two patients were placed on Antabuse (a placebo in reality) and were taught that their mind controls their drinking, not the drug.

Careful word usage is very important in any therapy, but is especially important in RBT. After some experience we came to understand that certain words are better used rigorously in the treatment of alcoholism: the words *want*, *need*, and *crave*. The word *want* refers to a cognitive process wherein a person (without felt craving) decides whether to drink or not by weighing alternatives, consequences, and his long-term best interest. Since this is a potentially rational process and capable of being influenced by other cognitions, it usually does not produce severe drinking problems and can be dealt with by using an RSA format.

The word *need* is used appropriately after someone has addicted himself to alcohol, i.e., it refers to physiological dependence defined as any process that will produce withdrawal symptoms. Thus if an alcoholic says, "I need a drink" and means that without one he will begin (or continue) to

---

[2] *You and Your Emotions* by Maxie C. Maultsby, Jr., M.D., and Allie Hendricks, M.A. $5.95 including postage. Available from: Rational Behavior Therapy Center, University of Kentucky, College of Medicine, 0084-M.C. Room N204A, Lexington, KY 40536.

suffer various withdrawal symptoms, then this is an appropriate usage. The obvious treatment intervention is detoxification.

The word *crave* is one that most people do not use but that would be useful to learn. It refers to the A–C, "thought shorthand," or, more accurately, a conditioned emotional reaction type of response. It is a felt (C) response of desiring to drink (cf. Russell and Brandsma, 1974). If this is a classically conditioned response to various stimuli (e.g., bar or friends), then the stimuli will be obvious upon interviewing. The treatment of choice is some sort of extinction process, i.e., put the patient (or have the patient put himself) in the presence of the stimuli but do not allow him to drink. If this is triggered by more of a cognitive process (i.e., craving occurs without the presence of external, classically conditioned stimuli), then it is probably an operant process. The person, for example, makes himself anxious and then finds alcohol reinforcing in anxiety reduction. The intervention here would be rational thinking to control the anxiety and the conscious use of other reinforcers or distractors.

At the inception of the project we devised an "ideal" treatment regimen for RBT: The patient would have five individual sessions and then be referred to a group for 10 individual and 10 group sessions running concurrently up to the 6-month point in treatment. Thereupon would come a 3-month hiatus, after which the patient would return for five individual sessions and enough group sessions to make a total of 40 treatment hours. As the project progressed it became obvious that our subjects were unable to follow this regimen; they would usually receive one individual session for a number of weeks until they finished 30 sessions or less, or dropped out.

RBT—Administered by a layman

The layman RBT treatment group was exactly the same as the professional RBT group in theory and technique. The only difference was the lack of professional training of the person who administered treatment. Essentially this man was a dedicated paraprofessional who took his responsibility seriously and may have had an advantage in his availability to his clients and his own understanding of dependence on chemicals.

At the outset of the project there were group sessions (usually three to five members at most), which would last for 2 hours. They would usually begin by the members discussing their weekly activities. Then the lay leader would give a mini-lecture on an aspect of rational theory or they would view a videotape together. Next the group would be questioned on the lecture or videotape material. After this discussion the lay leader would solicit problem situations and put one on a blackboard in the A-B-C format; the group would analyze and offer rational alternatives to the person whose problems was presented. Then the group leader would expound on the mistakes made in analysis that were related to his previous mini-lecture material.

After a few group sessions it was found that few clients would present problems of significance in the group setting. It was also difficult to bring together enough men for a group. Thus individual sessions were offered to those who were interested, and all clients indicated a preference for this verbally and behaviorally. From then on, group sessions were not held. Thus, this therapy was largely conducted on an individual basis. In the individual sessions there were basically three types of clients and interventions:

1. The very cooperative clients would bring in written homework assignments, which were reviewed, challenged, and polished. Then behavioral and cognitive assignments would be given for the next week.
2. Some refused to write but were sufficiently verbal to engage in a rational, Socratic dialogue. Both the first and second types would read the written materials. Cartoon handouts were given to all, but were especially aimed at lower intelligence clients. In addition, more standard prose handouts were given to the more verbal clients, and these provided topics for discussion before specific problems were focused upon. These two types also viewed at least four videotapes of Dr. Maultsby talking to a group of alcoholics and then discussed them with the lay therapist.
3. Some clients were resistant and recalcitrant in their verbal output and in doing homework. With these clients videotapes (usually all 11 in our series) were viewed together, and then they were questioned about them. Whenever possible, the material was related to their own lives.

The lay therapist reported that his previous drug dependency seemed to form a "common bond" with several of his clients. Some clients thought that the videotapes seemed to provide a measure of "professionalism" to their treatment. The tapes were a definite asset in this treatment even though they were used variably, depending on the individual.

Alcoholics Anonymous (AA)

There is probably wide variation in how AA groups are conducted across the country and world because of the social class and subcultural differences. However, given the experience and wide exposure of our two initial leaders, we believe that our group was conducted within the mainstream of AA practices and contained the "system of common norms" that unites AA units (cf. Leach et al., 1969).

Perhaps the essential elements of AA philosophy are that the sharing of common experiences, the mutual acceptance of one another as human beings, and the trusting in a "higher power" aid an individual in recovering from alcoholism. Although the procedures differ from group to group, a review of their approaches from a behavioral perspective would suggest a wide range of behavior change techniques, such as group therapy, religiou⁻ conversion and ideology, social reinforcement of abstinence behaviors, and modeling (cf. Brandsma, 1976).

Our group met once per week and tended to focus on persons present for the first time, but not to the exclusion of other members. The 12 steps of AA were used as the content focus for discussions. The men were made aware of the availability of "sponsor-friends" and were encouraged to ally themselves with one or more of their own choosing. Generally our patients seemed to neglect availing themselves of this opportunity, and the assignment of sponsors was not followed up on in this group. Beyond this description we are unable to be more specific. However, we are convinced that had tape recordings of these meetings been made, they could be easily discriminated from our other treatments.

The nature of scientific investigation did force some small changes in the usual AA norms. First, most of our clients came coerced from the court system and all were then randomly assigned to treatments. Thus they were not "free to choose" whether to have treatment or the type of treatment. However, a person's first visit to AA usually results from some form of "coercion," e.g. by a wife or boss. Second, participation was not anonymous because we kept attendance records, although this was an unobtrusive procedure. If a man's attendance was poor or nonexistent, he would be contacted at least once by a project social worker, reminded of the conditions of his parole, and encouraged to return. This type of "coercion" (in contrast to the "buddy system") is different than usual AA procedures. Our group did not develop a high degree of cohesiveness or a formalized buddy system as some do, nor did we offer other "services," as does Al-Anon. However, given our population, situation, and purposes, we believe this was a representative treatment effort within the AA framework.

Control Group

The control group was composed of 31 randomly assigned subjects. These individuals did not receive any active intervention on our part to treat them, but, of course, they could avail themselves of any of the treatment opportunities available in the community. Thus, this was a control for life experiences and "community treatment" of whatever kind actively utilized by the patient. We composed a mimeographed sheet listing community agencies that could provide services to alcoholics, a description of their services, their addresses, key people to contact, and their telephone numbers. This list included hospital alcoholism treatment programs, halfway houses, other AA groups, the comprehensive care center (Community Mental Health Center), and a private sanitarium. Our social workers encouraged the men to make use of these various services and even counseled them briefly on where they might begin seeking individualized help. However, the project social workers did not make arrangements for them. If the men made other contacts with us after this, we would only do more of the same, i.e., give them the sheet having a compilation of services on it and some brief counseling.

Termination Procedures

All professional therapists (insight and professional RBT groups) followed the same procedure in keeping their clients in therapy in order to control therapist motivation and behavior with regard to keeping people in treatment. After the first missed appointment the therapist was to contact his client by telephone and set up another appointment. If the client missed two scheduled appointments in a row, the therapist would inform the project social worker, who would send out a form letter to the client reminding him of his commitment and requesting that he contact his therapist to set up an appointment. After three sequentially missed appointments the therapist would inform the project social worker; then the social worker would make a personal visit to the man to try to induce him back into treatment. If this failed or the fourth scheduled session was missed, the patient was referred back to the court for appropriate action and was considered a dropout from the project.

Patients were terminated from treatment in one of these ways: by mutual consent with their therapist after having completed a minimum of 10 sessions, or when a total of 30 hours of therapy had been completed, or when 46 weeks had passed since their first therapy session—whichever occurred first. At the end of treatment the project social worker was to be notified by the therapist, whereupon the client was contacted and scheduled for outcome testing as soon as possible.

CRITERIA FOR INCLUSION IN TREATMENT SAMPLE

Psychotherapy is a learning process that takes a minimum amount of time (among other things) to accomplish its results. Our purpose was to give the therapies designated in this project a reasonable chance of success; one cannot fault the lack of a crop on a farmer who has just planted his seed. Thus we arbitrarily decided that a minimum application of psychotherapeutic treatment would be set at 10 sessions. (A study by Armor et al. (1978) has suggested that five might have been sufficient.) At the other extreme we were not interested for pragmatic research and efficiency reasons in testing treatments that would go on for years and create a special and probably unresolved dependency relationship to take the place of or exist with alcohol dependence. Thus we decided initially that a year was long enough time for significant learning and behavior change to occur if it ever was to be. This was later revised specifically to 46 weeks of treatment time. In summary then, all were included who had at least 10 sessions but not more than 30 in the 46 weeks that elapsed since their first treatment session.

We followed these criteria as closely as humanly possible, but, of course, some patients ran over the time period before having the outcome battery and a few others had over 30 sessions. Thus we made the following decision rules for the research sample: If the subject had 10 or more sessions but his treatment time was over 46 weeks, he could be included if his average number of sessions per week was 0.21 or greater, i.e., number of sessions/number of weeks > 0.21. The 0.21 figure as a minimum number was arrived at by dividing 10 sessions by 46 weeks. Thus it represents the number of fractional sessions per week that we had arbitrarily decided was minimum for therapeutic effectiveness.

CRITERIA FOR EVALUATION OF OUTCOME RESEARCH

At least in method, SHARP stands on the shoulders of those who have studied alcoholism and psychotherapy before. We are grateful to the scientific community for providing better guidelines for conducting research of this type over the last 10 years, and we attempted to avoid the pitfalls of past research efforts. The reader may evaluate to what extent we were successful.

Beyond the criteria of Hill and Blane (1967) in the field of alcoholism research, which we followed, an article by Luborsky et al. (1975) in psychotherapy outcome research listed 12 criteria with which to evaluate studies of this type. We list and paraphrase them here in order to allow one to briefly evaluate the success of our study. They are:

1. Patients should be assigned to groups in a controlled fashion such that there is comparability on important dimensions (such as initial severity of problem).
   a. One method is random assignment. It is risky and the groups must be examined at the beginning and end to determine whether dropouts have changed their comparable characteristics appreciably.
   b. A second and better method is the matching of the total groups on various characteristics.
   c. The third and best method is to match patients in pairs.
2. Studies of this type should use real patients.
3. The therapists for each group should be equally competent.
4. Therapists should be experienced.
5. Treatments should be valued equally.

6. Outcome measures should take into account the target goals of the treatment.
7. The outcome should be evaluated by independent measures, i.e., multivariate sources (cf. Foster et al., 1972, specifically for the field of alcoholism).
8. Information should be obtained about concurrent treatments, such as drugs.
9. Samples of treatment should be evaluated independently to see if they fit the designated treatment type.
10. Treatments should be equal in amount, length, and/or frequency.
11. Treatments should be given in reasonable amounts, appropriate to that form of treatment.
12. Sample size should be adequate—especially when random assignment is utilized.

In this and the following chapters the reader will note that this study usually conforms adequately and at times perhaps admirably to most of these criteria. It is to the instrumentation and results that we now turn our attention.

chapter 3
INSTRUMENTATION

This chapter presents the procedures used as dependent variables in the project with an accompanying rationale. We first turn our attention to the six procedures making up the screening battery.

MENTAL STATUS INTERVIEW

For ethical and practical reasons we wished to exclude individuals who had notable psychiatric symptomatology. For example, hallucinations might be the result of alcohol withdrawal or schizophrenia. It would not be appropriate or useful to treat people for alcoholism whose symptoms were expressions of other forms of psychopathology. Severe psychopathology would also make a successful outcome for alcoholism treatment very unlikely. Thus we constructed a brief, structured, mental status interview to assess information plus orientation, hallucinatory experiences, memory, thinking, speech, and affective disorder. The interviewer would probe for indications of inappropriate affect, mania, bizarre ideation, paranoia, and delusions, while assessing time and place orientation and clarity of speech. Appendix 4 reproduces the instrument in toto. At its end the interviewer was forced to make decisions on the appropriateness of the candidate from various aspects of his functioning. Another aspect usually included in mental status, appearance and manner, was not included because many of our *Ss* had recently spent the night in jail, and it did not seem relevant to our research goals.

We are not unaware of the potential problems with this kind of approach. Nathan and Harris (1975, p. 123) report:

> Although a mental status examination and a review of the patient's personal history are still the touch stones on which diagnosis, treatment, and research are based, these methods have long aroused controversy. The dispute revolves around their subjectivity and resultant potential for unreliability. In fact, research has shown that the age, sex, race, and socioeconomic status of the patient, the examiner, or both can affect the conclusions drawn from a psychiatric examination (Edwards, 1972; Routh and King, 1972). Research has also confirmed that experienced examiners do not always reach the same diagnostic or prognostic conclusions even when supplied with the same interview or observational data (Sandifer, 1972). Furthermore, patients do not always give the same amount and kind of information to all examiners (Edelman and Snead, 1972; Perrett, 1972).

Our usage of this instrument was further confounded (infrequently and mistakenly) by using it on respondents who were intoxicated. Nevertheless, the procedures were objective and useful in making decisions about our patients' suitability.

INTELLIGENCE TEST

Persons with a measured intelligence of less than 80 (above called "dull normal," below called "borderline" or a degree of retardation) have trouble performing adequately in many situations and do not learn new skills or concepts quickly. Because we wished to test the effects of psychotherapy, which is a learning process, we decided that this would be the cut-off for our sample. Beyond this, several of our outcome measures, particularly the MMPI, demanded this level of intellectual functioning in order to be valid.

The Kent (1946) Emergency Scale D was chosen because of its brevity, simplicity, and adequate correlation with the Wechsler-Bellvue. It consists of 10 free-response items and the item content focuses on areas of general knowledge. Responses are rated for completeness and quality. It was developed in 1932 to be used in jails and courthouses. Scale D was a reduced version of the original "Emergency Test" and was normed against 1700 adults.

Wright, MacPhee, and Cummings (1949) used this test on Army recruits and found a correlation with the Wechsler-Bellvue of 0.52. Mensh (1953) reported later studies showing correlations of 0.73 to the Wechsler-Bellvue and 0.74 to the Stanford-Binet. It is generally regarded as an adequate screening device for low intelligence. Of a possible 36 points a raw score of 21–23 corresponded to an IQ of 80 in Kent's norms. Therefore a score of 23 or better was considered a definite pass, a score of 20 a definite failure, and scores of 21 and 22 were borderline.

DRINKING QUESTIONNAIRE

In defining our sample it was critical to demonstrate that our Ss were "alcoholics" at the start of treatment. In order to eliminate individuals without apparent alcohol problems, an interview-administered questionnaire was developed. This was a 17-item inventory (see Appendix E) using a yes-no response format and drawing its content from the criteria list developed by the National Council on Alcoholism for usage in the diagnosis of alcoholism (cf. Ringer et al., 1977). The Council's diagnostic criteria are separated into two groups or "tracks" of symptoms: Track I, physiological and clinical, and Track II, behavioral, psychological, and attitudinal (see Appendix F). Each track contains major (obligatory) and minor (indicative) symptoms. The obligatory symptoms demand a diagnosis of alcoholism; the indicative symptoms raise suspicion but require collaborative data for the diagnosis. The National Council on Alcoholism (1972) recommends that:

> It is sufficient for the diagnosis of alcoholism if one or more of the major criteria are satisfied, or if several of the minor criteria in Tracks I and II are present. If one is making the diagnosis because of major criteria in one of the

tracks, he should also make a strong search for evidence in the other track. A purely mechanical selection of items is not enough; the history, physical examination, and other observations, plus laboratory evidence, must fit into a consistent whole to ensure a proper diagnosis. Minor criteria in the physical and clinical tracks alone are not sufficient, nor are minor criteria in the behavioral and psychological tracks. There must be several in both Track I and Track II area.

Our questionnaire was a mechanical selection of items, which the National Council suggests is insufficient. Unfortunately a more complex procedure was not feasible in our setting. Thus it is possible that the symptomatology assessed could have been due to psychopathology or organic brain dysfunction. However, our other testing procedures could cross-check this, and thus we believe that our screening procedure in toto was sufficient for diagnosing alcoholism.

Social workers administered the Drinking Questionnaire as the third instrument presented to respondents in the screening interview. When necessary, the items were read and explained to the Ss. The statistical results of this procedure are presented later, but, in general, individuals were diagnosed as alcoholic (and accepted into the program) if they had a score of 3 or greater on this test. This score indicated that probably at least one major and one minor criterion must have been passed (or three minor criteria). The National Council indicates that only one major criterion is necessary for the diagnosis of alcoholism.

DRAWING TEST

Fitzhugh, Fitzhugh, and Reitan (1965) reported that the performance of alcoholics on the Trail Making Test (TMT) (discussed in the next section) was better than that of individuals with diagnosed brain damage. However, Page and Linden (1974) compared the performance of alcoholics on the TMT to the norms given by Reitan and found that 71% of the alcoholics would be classifed as brain damaged. Thus interpreting the performance of an alcoholic on the TMT alone would be difficult and requires a corroborating instrument.

The Drawing Test consisted of two tasks removed from the Halstead-Wepman (1949) Aphasia Screening Test. These (along with others) were taken by Heimburger and Reitan (1961) to detect language dysfunction and distortion of spatial orientation. We used only two procedures taken from Heimburger and Reitan (1961) to determine whether our subjects' problems had an organic basis, since we were more interested in screening than localizing lesions. This was especially true for right hemisphere lesions since language (left hemisphere) functions would be assessed in our other procedures.

In the first part of the test we asked the respondent to copy one of three figures—a triangle, a square, and a Greek cross—without lifting his pencil from the paper. We then asked the respondent to read aloud the sentence "He shouted the warning" so that the examiner could determine if the respondent possessed any perceptual or expressive problems. The interviewers were free to readminister the task if they felt that the performance was not representative of the *Ss'* ability.

The rating of the second part of the test was graded more subjectively than the first part. The drawings were submitted to the following rules. The individual was said to have failed if the drawings contained any of the following elements: 1) an unrecognizable Gestalt; 2) corners that missed or overshot by more than $\frac{1}{8}$ inch; 3) a tremor measuring more than $\frac{1}{4}$ of an inch to either side of an imagined, visualized center line; or 4) drawings not of the same relative size as the originals.

Our norms for failure on this test were not taken from Heimburger and Reitan; only our procedures were taken from them. The rules for failure were our own. Taken in concert with the TMT we felt we had a reasonable screen for blatant organic dysfunction that would have interfered with our treatment procedures.

TRAIL MAKING TEST (TMT)

Seizures, blackouts, and tremors reported by our subjects could have been due to more permanent brain damage as well as the relatively transient effects of alcohol. Because of the deficits in learning and adaptive abilities usually found in individuals with organic brain dysfunction, and because these were not necessarily concomitants of (early) alcoholism, we wished to screen these individuals out of our sample. To this end, the TMT, a test that has been shown to be a valid indicator of organicity (Reitan, 1958b), was administered as the fifth instrument in the screening battery.

Briefly described, the TMT consists of two parts, each having 25 circles printed on a regular $8\frac{1}{2}'' \times 11''$ sheet of white paper. Part A has circles numbered 1–25; these must be connected in sequence by a pencil line as quickly as possible. Part B has circles numbered 1–13 and circles lettered A–L. The subject must connect the circles with a pencil line by alternating between numbers and letters in descending order (i.e., 1-A-2-B). The score is the time in seconds required by the subject to complete the task (Fitzhugh, Fitzhugh, and Reitan, 1960, p. 417). Reitan's administration procedure and norms were used to evaluate our results. There is extensive literature documenting the use of this instrument as a test for organicity and, more specifically, psychomotor speed, problem solving, set shifting, and adaptive ability (Klanknecht and Goldstein, 1972; Reitan, 1955, 1958a,b, 1962; Reitan and Davison, 1974; Reitan and Tarshes, 1959).

Cut-off times suggested by Reitan's normative data were set at 39 seconds for Part A and 91 seconds for Part B. These times set the amounts of false positives and false negatives approximately equal (23% on Part A, 15% on Part B). On Part B, for example, 15% of the controls would be mistakenly diagnosed as organic and 15% of the organic *Ss* would be mistakenly diagnosed as normal. Other times could have been arbitrarily chosen to reduce false positives or false negatives, but this would have increased total misclassification.

Several studies could be used to dispute our cut-off times. Fitzhugh et al. (1960, 1965), for example, compared the performances of normal, brain damaged, and hospitalized alcoholic individuals on a number of tasks measuring adaptive abilities. They postulated that the failure of alcoholic rehabilitation programs might be in part due to an impairment in adaptive abilities. Their 1960 data on the TMT indicated that the brain damaged and alcoholic samples were similar and the controls performed at a superior level. Their 1965 study replicated this, and showed an even greater difference between the performances of hospitalized brain damaged persons and alcoholics and those of controls. Page and Linden (1974) investigated the recovery of intellectual functioning in hospitalized alcoholics by administering a number of instruments at 2-week intervals for 8 weeks. Performance on most instruments was depressed at initial testing but improved with abstinence. The TMT improved significantly from the first testing to the last, but these scores, for the most part, would still classify the alcoholic as brain damaged. Indeed, they estimated that 71% of their sample would be classified in the brain damaged range compared to Reitan's norms (cf. Ayers et al., 1978).

Page and Linden's (1974) results are more meaningful to our study than those of Fitzhugh et al. (1960, 1965) because, although they used a hospitalized sample, they obtained measures over a long period of time. It is perhaps unfortunate that these results became available after our study was underway. However, none of these studies presents new normative data nor suggests a set of cut-off times more appropriate for use in our context. Thus in the absence of more standardized guidelines the use of the established norms seems reasonable. Furthermore, our awareness of the cut-off problem from the Fitzhugh studies resulted in less weight being placed on the TMT performance when a decision for inclusion was made; the respondent could fail the TMT and still be included in the sample if all other criteria were met successfully.

Reading Test

The sixth and last instrument administered during the screening interview was an abbreviated form of the Gray Oral Reading Test (1955). Interviewers instructed the respondent to read paragraph seven "carefully and as well as they possibly can." The time required to read the paragraph and the number of errors made were recorded by the interviewer. Errors consisted of: 1) mispronunciation; 2) repeating two words in a row, i.e., "The sun had sunk—had sunk behind . . ."; 3) omissions; and 4) substitutions. If the respondent took longer than 40 seconds or had more than two errors, he failed paragraph seven and was asked to read paragraph six, a simpler paragraph. Then it was noted if he had read this paragraph at a level sufficient to pass the criteria.

We planned to use this procedure to screen out Ss who could not read at a sixth grade level. Attainment of sixth grade level was necessary in order to fill out other instruments (such as the MMPI) and benefit from some of the treatment materials (in the RBT or AA treatment, for example). Unfortunately, we did not communicate a decision rule clearly to our screening social worker. The result was that the test was given and data collected, but the data were not used to screen out anybody. When we discovered this, we developed an oral, tape-recorded form of the MMPI to be given to our patients who had trouble reading. However, in the analysis of these data, we employed a system of scoring based on certain assumptions made in order to estimate the reading ability. This procedure and its assumptions are reported in Appendix G. The results are reported in Chapter 4.

FINGER PAIN TOLERANCE

Petrie's (1967) investigations of individual differences in sensitivity (perceptual reactivity) to pain suggested that alcohol increased tolerance for physical discomfort only among those individuals most sensitive to pain, the "augmenters." Petrie suggested (1967, p. 91) that augmenters would be more likely to become alcoholics, and we thought that this might have relationship to outcome in therapy even though its relationship to personality correlates is equivocal at best (Brown, Fader, and Barber, 1973).

In order to investigate the relationship between pain tolerance (believed to be similar to pain threshold measures by Brown et al., 1973) and alcoholism more thoroughly, an instrument (see Figure 2) was designed similar to that described by Forgione and Barber (1971). (For this instrument we used their specifications but produced pressure mechanically rather than electrically.) This instrument induced pressure pain on the dorsal surface of the index finger of the dominant hand. A pressure of 1330.8 grams was placed between the first and second knuckle after the following instructions were given:

> "This is a measure of pain tolerance. I am going to place the index finger of your dominant hand in this device and time how long you will allow the blade

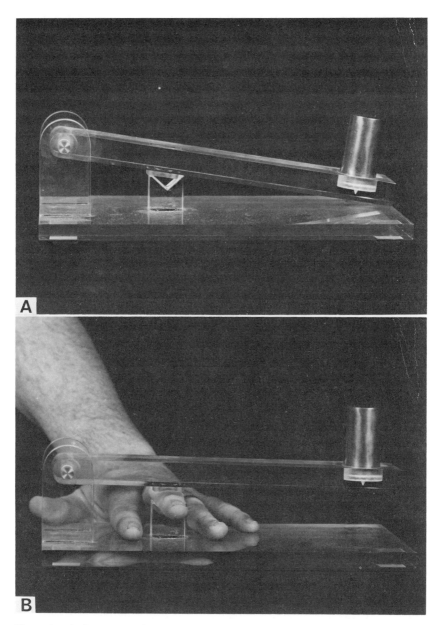

Figure 2. A, Instrument that tests pain tolerance. B, Instrument places 1330.8 grams of pressure between first and second knuckles. Subjects are asked to tolerate the pain for as long as they can.

on your finger. Please try to tolerate the pain as long as you can; then tell me when you do not wish to continue. Do you understand?"

Aspects of the instructions could be repeated or explained using these words, if necessary. If the man went beyond 3 minutes, the procedure was stopped and the 3-minute time recorded.

Specifically in this measure we planned to look at: 1) pain tolerance in alcoholics, 2) relationships between personality factors and this pain tolerance measure, 3) pain tolerance and craving, and 4) the use of this measure of pain tolerance as a possible predictor of treatment outcome.

BREATHALIZER

When subjects would return for follow-up at 3 and 12 months after treatment termination, they would be administered a Breathalizer test to check their blood level of alcohol. They would not be previously aware that this would occur. Standard procedures in administration of the Smith and Wesson Model 900A Breathalizer[1] were employed and the results recorded.

A complete record of the instruments used and their points of intervention into the process is provided in Table 9 of Chapter 4.

BEHAVIORAL MEASURES

Working for Money and Alcohol

Working for money and alcohol was chronologically a continuation of the predictor paradigm, which is described on p. 52. (See Appendix H for instructions and Figure 3.) Briefly, Ss were given four 2-minute periods to work for money or its equivalent in alcohol by pressing a button. The Ss were asked to press the button at least 15 times in each period to make sure they understood the workings of the apparatus and to overcome whatever inertia effects there might be. At the end of each period the person was given a choice of whether to pocket his money or drink an equivalent amount of his favorite alcoholic beverage, depending on whether he had been working for alcohol or money. These choices and the amounts earned were recorded. There has been no previous research on this apparatus, although a similar type was employed by Ludwig, Wikler, and Stark (1974). We used the relative amounts of work as a behavioral measure(s) of a person's desire for or relatedness to alcohol, and correlated this with various outcome criteria as a predictor and also as a change measure since this procedure was given at outcome and at 3- and 12-month follow-ups.

---

[1] Smith and Wesson Electronics Company, Meridan Road, Eatontown, NJ 07724.

Drinking Alcohol Offered by Experimenter

Each subject had the opportunity to accept a "free" drink in the predictor paradigm and twice to accept the drink he had "earned" in the button-pressing paradigm. On each of these occasions we registered whether or not he did drink the beverage.

SELF-REPORT MEASURES

Demographic Questions

Behavior is a function of many variables, including role and normative expectations. Some of the most influential sources of these expectations are groups that individuals belong to that can be identified by demographic characteristics. It is quite probable that age and social class have an effect on treatment outcomes. Investigators have found that success in alcohol treatment programs is related to age (older individuals improve more), occupation (professional and skilled laborers improve more), and social stability (those married and employed improve more).

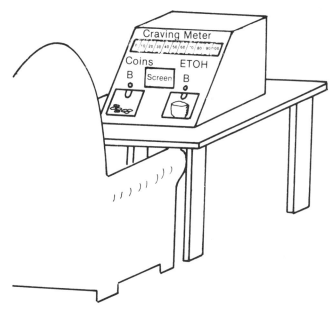

Figure 3.   Craving and work panel. The Craving Meter is on top of the work panel. The letter "B" on the drawing designates the location of the buttons. (Manufactured by BRS—Foringer Division of Technical Services, 5451 Holland Drive, Beltsville, Maryland 20705.)

Although many current programs are open to all applicants, the question of which individuals will improve on what dimension is still important because of the frequent necessity and desire to devote therapeutic resources in the most efficient manner. Demographic characteristics have been focused on by a (small) number of investigations attempting to see what variables correlate with improvement and thus develop a prognostic index. If they would work, they could be a more efficient way to make treatment decisions.

Tables 1 and 2 indicate the programs and their large variety of variables, which have been examined in relationship to treatment outcome. Table 2 indicates that these relationships tend to be inconsistent. Two variables, however, marital status and employment stability, correlate consistently with improvement. A composite variable, often labeled social or personal stability, is also related consistently to positive outcome (Gerard and Saenger, 1966; Kissin, Rosenblatt, and Machover, 1968; Mayer and Myerson, 1965). This variable usually includes marital status and employment stability (as well as others) or is postulated as the moderating variable behind these two (Goldfried, 1969; Zax, Marsey, and Biggs, 1961). In addition a subjective variable, high motivation, based either on therapists or interviewer estimate or inferred from self-referral, has been found to relate to improvement after treatment.

In order to assess the demographic characteristics of the individuals involved in our project, a questionnaire (see Appendix H) was developed. The questionnaire was designed to obtain information on eight aspects of the client:

1. Current socioeconomic status
2. Employment history
3. Marital status and sexual adjustment
4. Psychiatric care history
5. Arrest record
6. Current drug usage
7. Drinking history and current drinking patterns
8. Presence of psychiatric or alcohol problems among blood relatives

Specifically, these categories were handled in the following manner:

1. Hollingshead's (1957) two-factor index of social position involving education and occupation was employed to assess current socioeconomic status.
2. Employment history was obtained through a series of free-response items, which inquired about the nature of the current job (full- or part-time), the length of time employed on the current job, the type of job held for the longest period of employment, and the number of job changes in the past year and in the last 6 years.

Table 1. Characteristics of programs that have attempted to identify factors to predict improvement in alcoholism treatment programs

Source	Treatment facility	Treatment	Outcome measure	Data source
			Program characteristics	
Mindlin (1959)	Outpatient clinic	Unidentified form of therapy, presumably counseling	Improvement in drinking, work adjustment, social adjustment, and emotional adjustment	Unclear
Zax et al. (1961)	Rochester Outpatient Clinic	Medication	Number of sessions	Treatment records
Kissin et al. (1968)	Ward and outpatient clinic	Drugs, drugs and psychotherapy, inpatient treatment, control	Drinking abstinent or almost, and improvement in social and vocational areas for 6 months before interview	Interview by social worker 1 year after registration
Goldfried (1969)	Rochester Outpatient Clinic	Medication and psychotherapy	Changes in drinking behavior, home, and social life and functioning at work	Change ratings based on preassessment interview on prior year's functioning and follow-up interview at 4 and 8 months, interview content rated by judges for improvement
Mayer and Myerson (1965)	Outpatient clinic	Unspecified treatment administered by non-psychiatric physicians and social workers	Changes in drinking and improvement in work and marital relations	Evaluation of treatment records
Gerard and Saenger (1966)	A number of outpatient clinics	Drug and psychotherapy	Whether drinking is abstinent or controlled	Six-month follow-up interview

Table 2.   Client variables examined as predictors of client improvement in alcoholism treatment programs

Client variables[a]	Source					
	Mindlin (1959)	Zax et al. (1961)	Kissin et al. (1968)	Goldfried (1969)	Mayer and Myerson (1965)	Gerard and Saenger (1966)
Marital status (married and with wife)	*	*	NS	*	*	*
Employment stability (steady job)	*	—	*	*	—	*
Employment type (professional, clerical, skilled)	*	NS	*	—	—	*
Social stability[b] (MS +, ES +, others)	—	—	*	NS	*[c]	*[d]
Motivation (I rating)	*	*	*	*	—	—
Referral (self or wife)	—	*	*	—	—	—
Age (over 40)	NS	NS	*	—	—	NS[e]
Education (some college)	NS	NS	*	*	—	NS
Religion	NS	NS	*[f]	—	—	—
Race	—	—	*[g]	—	—	NS
Arrest record	*[h]	—	NS[i]	—	—	—
AA affiliation	—	—	NS	—	—	*[j]
Drinking	—	—	*[k]	*[l]	—	—

Variables found to relate significantly to success or failure indentified by (*); (—) denotes variables not assessed and (NS) indicates a nonsignificant relation found.

[b] Social stability is mainly comprised of marital status (MS) and employment status (ES).

[c] Significant difference only for low status clients.

[d] Both total score and components significant. Gerard and Saenger note however that effect may be confounded by a therapist bias against low stability clients.

[e] Often cited as finding older improved more, however, difference was nonsignificant.

[f] Confounded with race and stability, Negroes were low stable, Protestant, and improved significantly less.

[g] When controlled for social stability difference is nonsignificant.

[h] Five arrests or less improved more than 20 or more.

[i] Two arrests or less compared to all else.

[j] Only for a sample of matched success and failures.

[k] Binge drinkers improved more.

[l] Number of weeks abstinent in prior year.

3. Questions about the current marital status and number of times married were asked. Sexual adjustment was measured by the Abbreviated Scale of Premorbid Sexual Adjustment (Harris, 1975).
4. Psychiatric history was obtained by asking the client about any involvement in counseling and outpatient or inpatient treatment for alcohol-related problems.
5. The arrest record involved a self-report of the number and type of arrests, such as the number of traffic violations in the past year and the number of traffic accidents in the last 5 years.
6. Current drug usage was recorded in response to the question, "What drugs (besides alcohol) have you used in the past 2 weeks?"
7. Drinking pattern and history were assessed by 22 questions taken from a questionnaire employed at Mendota State Hospital Alcoholism Research Project (Stein, Newton, and Bowman, personal communication).
8. A checklist was provided for the patient to indicate which of his blood relatives, if any, had been diagnosed or treated for psychiatric illness or had a history of alcoholism.

Problem Checklist

A brief 45-item checklist was developed (Brandsma, 1972c) to be put to several uses (See Appendix I), one of which was to get a frequency count of expressed problems. It was administered only at the initial testing battery. Its uses were to be: 1) to see if there was a bias in the random assignment of *Ss* to groups, i.e., one group getting more expressed problems than another (there were no differences), and 2) to provide the therapist with a means (should he decide to use it) of evaluating and beginning therapy. No research was done on this form before its use, and its use was not extensive. The interested reader can consult Mooney and Gordon (1950) for an extensive treatment of the development and usage of problem checklists.

Craving and Withdrawal Question

The Craving and Withdrawal Questionnaire was used at the initial, outcome, and 6- and 12-month follow-up points as both a predictor and change measure. Ludwig and Wikler (1974) have argued that craving is a complementary but distinct concept from the related notion of loss of control, and that an individual's perception of this may be a valuable predictor of his response to varying kinds of treatment. Although the concept of craving is intuitively appealing and often implicitly or explicitly used to explain continued consumption or resumption of drinking (Jellinek et al., 1955), few investigators have examined the relationship between subjective craving and actual behavior or ability to modify alcohol intake.

In our study we used the Ludwig-Stark Drinking and Craving Questionnaire (DCQ) to explore those relationships (Ludwig, Wikler, and Stark, 1974). Within this instrument are three scales focusing on Ludwig and Wikler's conception of craving and loss of control. We employed 10 questions from their Craving Experiences Scale, wherein a situation is described and the respondent is asked to rate his intensity of response on a 4-point scale, and nine questions related to drinking habits as our craving questions. We also included 13 questions to assess the frequency and intensity of alcohol withdrawal symptoms. For example, "Have you had a convulsion (fit) when sobering up?" The respondent chooses one of three alternatives: no; yes, sometimes; yes, frequently (see Appendix J).

The validity and usefulness of these specific conceptions are not established; they are interesting, intuitively plausible hypotheses. However, this instrumentation generated by these ideas seemed valid superficially and interesting enough to attempt to use as empirical predictors.

PREDICTOR PARADIGM

For this study a procedure called the "predictor paradigm" was developed to provide several different kinds of measures. The orientation and instructions for this procedure (read to patients by audiotapes) and other relevant materials for its administration are available from the authors, and Figure 3 shows a drawing of the apparatus. Briefly, each subject would sit in front of the alcohol-money machine and be requested to watch the small screen in front of him after the GSR electrodes were attached. Then 20 words (15 neutral—4 alchol related) would be flashed on the screen for 10 seconds and GSC would be recorded. This was the first part of the exercise. Next the subject would be asked to uncover a shot glass full of his favorite alcoholic beverage. His GSC would be recorded. Then he would be asked to rate his craving by pushing 1 of 10 buttons labeled from 0 to 100. Zero was defined as "no desire at all for a drink right now" and 100 as an "overpowering need for a drink right now." The subject was given opportunity to drink the beverage and his behavior was recorded. The electrodes were then removed. This procedure was thus to provide psychophysiological, subjective, and behavioral data concerning a person's response to alcohol. It was used at initial testing and at the 12-month follow-up as an outcome measure.

OUTCOME MEASURES (BOTH PRE-POST AND POST ONLY)

Minnesota Multiphasic Personality Inventory (MMPI)

Since its publication in 1943 (Hathaway and McKinley), the MMPI has had an extensive and useful history in psychological research. The reader is referred to Dahlstrom, Welsh, and Dahlstrom (1972) and Butcher (1969) for up-to-date summaries of its usefulness in various applications, and to Clapton (1978) for specific alcoholism application. We agreed with Bergin (1971, p. 260) that "despite some (previously iterated) deficits, no other paper-pencil measure of psychopathology based on self-report offers anything better to the researcher."

We hoped to put our research efforts into the context of previous data, and the MMPI provided a way to compare results because of its extensive usage. Beyond this there are over 160 scales that have been developed from the MMPI in various research contexts. Besides the usual clinical scales, we decided a priori to look at four other scales: 1) In several factor analyses, three or four consistent factors have been found for the MMPI (Finney, 1966; Welsh, 1952). Factor A, thought to measure anxiety and general emotional upset, was predicted to drop as the individual became less superficial and in touch with his real problems. 2) Factor C, Stability-compulsivity vs. unpredictability, was predicted to start low and increase with treatment. 3) Responsibility (conversely an index of manipulativeness) would be predicted to increase. 4) Dependency would be predicted to fall. 5) Alcoholism scales would be expected to decrease with treatment. Several other scales would be investigated with regard to correlations with other instruments and in their own right, but no a priori predictions were made for these. The Minnesota norms were utilized for the clinical scales and Finney's Kentucky Norms were used for all other scales. The Kentucky norms, collected in the late 1960s, are based on a sample of 1024 males and 1024 females, and are utilized as normalized T scores (Finney, personal communication).

For those subjects who were accepted but unable to read proficiently enough to take the MMPI in a reasonable time period, we developed an audiotape reproduction of the MMPI items. The Ss would listen to the item and then indicate on their answer sheet whether their response was true or false.

Behavior Rating Scale (BRS, BRS-R)

In addition to the somatic problems caused by the prolonged ingestion of alcoholic beverages, persons with alcohol problems concomitantly have tremendous difficulty in maintaining social adjustment. This is exhibited in employment instability, incarceration periods, monetary mismanagement, and variability in interpersonal relationships. If alcoholism treatment is to be successful, it must address itself to these areas as well as that of sobriety.

At the outset we outlined ambitious goals for our treatments and follow-up, i.e., would strive for abstinence from alcohol where appropriate and more adaptive functioning in work, family, and social situations. Thus it would be appropriate to measure drinking pattern and consumption as well as indicators of adequate social functioning. In many ways then, the

BRS became the bedrock instrument of our study to assess its success. This instrument was given at pre- and posttreatment and at each follow-up period, a total of six times. Besides this, a similar form was given to a relative or close associate of the subject if possible at outcome and 6-month follow-up as a cross-validation procedure.

For our study we chose the BRS (Stein, Newton, and Bowman, 1975) to evaluate changes in: a) social relationships, b) employment record, and c) drinking pattern. These investigations drew their question content from Ludwig et al. (1970) and Horn and Wanberg's (1969) work and developed forced-response items in each of the above areas. The first four sections of the BRS can be found in Appendix K and the drinking section in Appendix L.

BRS   The initial version of this instrument was developed by Ludwig et al. (1970) using a free-response interview format. Separate interviews were administered to the patient and a relative 1 week before therapy and were repeated 3 months following treatment. These responses were rated on scales designed to reflect the degree of social adjustment. In this original study the correlation between the patient's report and his relative's report on the first administration was only moderate ($0.31 \leq r \leq 0.66$); the relative's report judged the patient to be in much worse shape than the patient's report. The instrument was thought to have a large degree of face validity, but they also examined construct validity by comparing ratings of social adjustment made by a psychiatrist and social worker from an interview to ratings made from BRS data. In this regard correlations ranged from 0.63 to 0.99, depending on the subscale of the BRS examined.

Stein et al. (1975) eliminated the free-response format and thus the need for raters to make an assessment of social adjustment. In their study, which assessed the effects of detoxification and inpatient or patient care, no differences were found between groups. They believed that this was because of the ineffectiveness of the treatments rather than the insensitivity of the BRS. This inferential validation was based on five points:

1. The spread in the BRS total score distribution indicates that there was inter-subject discrimination.
2. The self-report data were restricted to discrete, countable behaviors.
3. The self-report data that could be verified corresponded sufficiently to actual records.
4. The measure of drinking behavior correlated moderately with the total BRS score.
5. The groups involved did show improvement on this measure even if they did not discriminate from each other, and this improvement held at the end of 13 months.

Stein et al. (1975) concluded:

> Thus although we have conducted no rigorous analyses of validity or reliability, the BRS was carefully conceived, contained objective items, and was pretested. All of the factors discussed above support our confidence that the BRS is a reasonably reliable and valid instrument (p. 252).

SHARP employed the Stein et al. (1975) revision of the BRS; our only changes were minor deletions of nonapplicable items.

Drinking Indices   Some of the most critical measures conceptually of our program's effectiveness were the indices of alcohol consumption. Even if abstinence was not achieved, the nature of our client population would at least require a significant reduction in quantity to achieve other goals in their lives. Despite the absolutely essential nature of this measure, it remains one of the most difficult to assess reliably and validly because investigators are forced to rely on post hoc self-report rather than direct observation. SHARP utilized a modification (Bowman, Stein, and Newton, 1975) of one of the more frequently used measures of drinking behavior, the Calahan, Cisin, and Crossley (1969) Quantity-Frequency-Variability Index.

The original Quantity-Frequency-Variability Index (Q-F-V Index) was developed by Cahalan et al. (1969) for their National Survey of American Drinking. Each respondent was asked to indicate how frequently and in what quantity he consumed wine, beer, and hard liquor. The quantity never exceeded six drinks per day and was expressed in "glasses" or "drinks." Bowman et al. (1975) modified the Q-F-V Index for an alcoholic population in hopes that it would be more sensitive to changes in drinking pattern.

> For several reasons we found it necessary to modify this system: (1) Our target population consisted of problem drinkers admitted to a state hospital, which meant we were examining a skewed distribution of drinking behaviors within which we had to make useful dinstinctions; (2) because the study was experimental with a limited population to draw upon, we needed measures of change that were as sensitive as possible; (3) the majority of our other measures were amendable to parametric analyses, so we desired an index of drinking behavior that could be handled as an interval scale as well as reduced to a typology. These considerations led us to develop the volume-pattern (V-P) index (p. 1160).

Using the Bowman et al. modified protocol we were able to generate and use three indices of drinking behavior: the Q-F-V Index, the Volume-Variability (V-V Index), and the Quantity-Volume (Q-V) Index (see Appendix M for a full explanation and description). Bowman et al. (1975) also developed a complicated Volume-Pattern Index, which we did not employ because neither our interviewers or respondents understood it, and because it proved to be of little empirical utility in their studies.

Table 3.   Arrest records as an outcome measure

Study	Number of Ss	Time period	Results in improvement (rounded %)
Bowen and Androes (1968)	79	1-year follow-up	85% had no arrests
Brown (1963)	40	4 years of treatment	65% had not returned to prison
Clancy (1961)	12	6 months of treatment	100% had no arrests
Clancy, Vanderhoof, and Campbell (1967)	42	1-year follow-up	86% had no court convictions
Clancy, Vornbrock, and Vanderhoof (1965)	59	1-year follow-up	88% had no court convictions
Connecticut Review (The chronic drunkenness offender in Connecticut, 1957)	21	Unreported	100% had no arrests during treatment
Cowen (1954)	63	6-year follow-up	97% had no arrests
Davies, Shepard, and Myers (1956)	49	2-year follow-up	16%
Ditman and Crawford (1966)	472	3-6 month periods	23%-32%
Ditman et al. (1967)	301	1 year of follow-up	0 Arrests 1 Arrest AA 31% 22 PT 32% 28 No treatment 44% 19
Esterly (1971)	90	3½-6 years including at least one of treatment	Treated group had fewer arrests than before treatment and less than control group
Faillace, Vourlekis, and Szara (1970)	12	2-year follow-up	11 of 12 not arrested
Ferguson (1970)	115	18 months of treatment	31% had no arrests, 23% had only one arrest
Gallant et al. (1968a)	19	1 year after intake	Involuntary—80% not violated parole Voluntary—22% not violated parole
Gallant et al. (1968b)	84	6 months of treatment	5% had no arrests
Hoffer (1967)	14	49 months after intake	86% had no arrests
Khoury and Pearson (1961)	Unreported	6 months in treatment	58% improved on previous 6-month arrest record
Kimmel (1971)	141	"Follow-up"—time unreported	94% were not in prison

Study	N	Follow-up	Results
Kurland (1968)	378	18 months follow-up	72% had no drunkenness arrests, 78% had no disorderly conduct arrests
Lal (1969)	38	12 weeks of treatment	97% were not arrested
Maier and Fox (1958)	16	3–6 months of treatment	69% improved their number of arrests
Mindlin (1960)	77	1–2 years of follow-up	18% had no arrests, 44% improved their number of arrests
Moore and Ramseur (1960)	91	42 months follow-up	86% remained out of prison
Myerson et al. (1961)	20	Unreported	70% remained out of prison
Norvig and Nielson (1956)	221	2¾–5¼ years follow-up	89% had no criminal offenses
Pittman and Tate (1969)	255	1-year follow-up after inpatient discharge	Average 65% with no arrests
Pokorny, Miller, and Cleveland (1968)	88	1-year follow-up	84% not in trouble with law
Prothro (1961)	469	Up to 3 years of aftercare	95% were not in prison
Robson, Paulus, and Clarke (1965)	155	10–46 months initial to follow-up	25% of treated and controls were improved in liquor-related offenses
Rohan (1970)	99	Average 10.4 months after input discharge	85% were not arrested
Sheuerman et al. (1961)	49	6 months after compulsory treatment	Drop in average number of arrests compared to the 6 months of preceding treatment
Smart et al. (1966, 1967)	30	6 months after treatment	Pre-post treatment in number of Ss ($N = 10$)

	Incarcerations	Drunkenness convictions	Impaired driving
Control	3 → 1	2 → 1	1 → 0
Ephedrine	3 → 2	8 → 4	1 → 0
LSD	3 → 3	4 → 6	1 → 0

Study	N	Follow-up	Results
Yapalater (1965)	169	5–8½ years after prison release	62% were not recidivist

The authors are indebted to C. D. Emrick for supplying bibliographic references for this table (personal communication, 1977).

Arrest Records

The use of arrest records as a measure of outcome is a rather gross but socially significant measure of behavior change. Table 3 provides a fairly complete listing of the use of this measure as an outcome indicator in previous studies. Our study collected both self-report data and more "objective" data on arrests. While our study was being conducted, Sobell, Sobell, and Samuels (1974) reported that self-reported arrests were valid enough to be used. This is encouraging to all previous research, but it still seems a good idea to use both if accurate data can be obtained.

The use of police records as an objective measure of arrest record would seem on the surface to have the advantages of being reliable, valid, and unobtrusive. Although it was unobtrusive and we were able to get these records for the year before and after treatment as well as for the time during treatment, its reliability and validity can be questioned for the following reasons:

1. It was found that the police were not always reliable or consistent in their reporting.
2. During our study the city and county governments merged and thus their record-keeping systems also were integrated. Before merging one was computerized and the other was not; there were probably distortions and lost data in this process.
3. Other counties were involved with a different system of records, which had to be negotiated.
4. Subjects often gave aliases or different forms of their name, for example, C. R. Smith, Charlie Smith, C. Robert Smith.

Given this problematic situation we did what was possible and received excellent cooperation from the authorities. One person was hired to collect these records. Because he left town with the job three-fourths completed, another was hired who finished the job and cross-checked the first person's work. Only verifiable information was used. A computer print-out of all people with the same last name as our clients' and their known aliases was obtained. These were cross-checked for name, initials, birth date, race, and with all other data sources. If there was convergence for a given individual (for example, the birth dates and initials matched), then the arrests during the appropriate period were summated. Given these procedures, we are fairly certain of the verifiability of our data; its veridicality is still open to question.

Therapist Evaluation Form

At the termination of therapy for the experimental subjects in the professional groups the therapists were asked to fill out an evaluation form concerning their perception of their clients. The items on this form closely paralleled the BRS format and content in order that we might study the correspondence between the two and give the therapists specific areas to evaluate. Therapists were asked to note specific social, legal, and economic events on a 5-point rating from poor to excellent, and were given opportunity for comments at the end of each section. On the last page of this form two questions were asked: Has the patient's major complaint been resolved? Have problematic attitudes related to this area improved? This form can be found in Appendix N.

chapter 4
RESULTS

Over a 4-year period a total of 532 subjects were screened for entrance into the research project. The purpose of the screenings was to eliminate persons who were retarded, psychotic, organically impaired, or not alcoholic. Analyses of the interviewing and test results upon completion of accepting *Ss* indicated that we were largely successful in screening out those whom we suspected could not benefit from psychotherapeutic intervention.

In order to check on our social worker's ability to screen accurately, we reanalyzed the Mental Status Interview protocols. Three experienced clinical psychologists read all the responses for the three free-response items: What does religion mean? What does marriage mean? Why do things happen in the world? These were determined to be appropriate or inappropriate with regard to the presence of delusions. If two of the three clinicians agreed within the 4-point rating system (inappropriate vs. three degrees of appropriate), that score was assigned. If the three did not agree, the scores were averaged. Beyond this the computer was programmed to make judgments on the basis of the answers to the questions concerning hallucinations and recent and remote memory loss. By and large this second set of analyses (called "objective") was in compliance with the social worker's judgments, although it tended to be more harsh. Where differences exist it is difficult to decide if it is because of the human factors or the methodology of the "objective" ratings. In any event these results are reported to make the reader aware of the variance because of the instruments or procedures used (employing human judgment).

Of the 532 that were screened, 260 were accepted for treatment assignment. Of these, 184 were from the courts and 76 were self-referred or referred from other agencies. Several analyses were performed to see what difference existed between those who were accepted and those who were rejected. Table 4 has a summary of the statistically significant results. For continuous data, comparisons were made with the *t* statistic: for categorical data chi square was employed. The number of subjects varied for each analysis depending on the amount of missing data; sample populations varied between 262 and 197 for the accepted *Ss*, and 226 and 119 for the rejected *Ss*. Significant differences are reported in Table 4.

No differences between the groups were found on measures of:

1. Ounces of ethanol consumed per day
2. Subjective ratings (social worker) of delusions
3. Subjective ratings (social worker) of hallucinations
4. Objective ratings (experienced judges) of delusions

Table 4. Accepted vs. rejected Ss comparisons

Index	Accepted Ss	Descriptive and clinical significance
Drinking		
Major physiological	Greater	Mean differences small but large sample size
Major behavioral + attitudinal	Greater	makes statistically significant
Minor behavioral + attitudinal	Greater	
Total drinking	Greater	
Intelligence		
Kent IQ	Greater	92 vs. 78—Accepted Ss averaged 13 points higher
Organicity		
Trails A	Faster	Rejects were twice as slow
Trails B	Faster	Rejects were almost twice as slow
Combined impairment index	Less impaired	27% of accepted were impaired vs. 88% of rejects
Ratings of recent memory	Less impaired	16% of accepted were impaired vs. 40% of rejects
Ratings of remote memory	Less impaired	13% of accepted were impaired vs. 34% of rejects
Objective remote memory	Less impaired	11% of accepted were impaired vs. 40% of rejects
Demographic		
Age	Younger	3 years younger
Education	More	3 years more education
Employment	More	69% accepted currently employed vs. 58% of rejects
Marital status	More	40% of accepted were married vs. 29% of rejects
Sixth grade reading level	More	82% of accepted could read vs. 48% of rejects

$N = 260$ maximum for the accepted Ss; 226 maximum for the rejected Ss.

5. Objective ratings (computer scoring) of hallucinations
6. Objective ratings (computer scoring) of recent memory loss

The populations, means, standard deviations, and levels of significance for these analyses are found in Appendix O.

Taken in concert these results have several interesting aspects. On all of the self-report drinking indices the accepted *Ss* were willing to admit to more pyschological, behavioral, and attitudinal problems connected with drinking. Mean differences here were small and significance was reached because of large sample size. Given the other, more severe impairments of those rejected, it is interesting that they had a tendency to not report aspects of their drinking problem. Perhaps this occurred because of failing memory or a need to deny the seriousness of their afflictions.

Generally, those who were accepted by these measures were brighter (higher IQ, educational level, reading level), younger, more socially involved (employed, married), and less organically impaired. This total population seems to be representative of the "revolving door" alcoholic court cases in our cities. They do not seem to be overtly psychiatrically impaired in terms of obvious psychopathology (hallucinations and delusions), but there is a tremendous amount of organic brain damage indicated directly and perhaps indirectly (employment). Having less education would seem to indicate that those rejected started life with less intelligence or opportunity, but the ravages of alcoholism have surely taken their toll on their brains as well as their bodies and families. This is a sad commentary on the effects of alcohol abuse and the social response.

Examination of the differences between the social workers' judgments and the more "objective" procedures showed that on each measure the "objective" procedures indicated proportionately more pathology and impairment than did the social workers. However, there were no significant differences between these two sets of analyses except on the recent memory variables. It is possible that the clinical judgment of the social worker at the end of the interview was influenced by impressions received incidentally throughout the procedure (usually a positive halo effect), whereas the computer only looked at the yes-no responses to three specific questions, which ask the subject if he was forgetful in different ways. In any event, the social worker saw less impairment generally, and in the case of recent memory saw the rejected subjects as being much more impaired than those accepted, whereas the computer did not (see Appendix O).

DESCRIPTION OF SAMPLE

Of the 260 accepted for treatment, 197 initiated treatment and 104 completed at least 10 sessions and took at least some of the outcome measures.

Three factors account for most of the 63 individuals lost between screening and treatment initiation:

1. Individuals who lived out of town and were unable to commute regularly for treatment
2. Potential clients who were involved at that time in other alcohol treatment programs, which prevented their participation in the present study
3. Respondents who were unwilling to accept the random nature of treatment assignment and the possibility of assignment to a nontreatment control condition

The group of 104 constituted our treatment sample. The following data speak to the issue of whether those men could be considered alcoholics. Table 5 indicates the total ounces of ethanol consumed per day by drinking beer, wine, and liquor; 97 *Ss* admitted to drinking these amounts for more than 1 day in a row.

Of our 104 treated *Ss*, 79 admitted to having blackouts, 56 had been advised by a doctor to stop drinking, 46 had lost at least one job because of drinking, and 60 had serious marital problems related to drinking. Probably because of our usage of court populations, 97 reported on intake to having been arrested for an alcohol-related offense at least once in their lives. Sixty-four admitted to drinking before noon and 51 admitted to attempting to hide their drinking, but 40 claimed that they could stop drinking after two drinks.

Another way of assessing whether these men were truly alcoholics is to look at their responses to our questionnaire based on the criteria of the National Council on Alcoholism. Table 5 shows the number of symptoms indicated by each subject.

As indicated in Table 5, all *Ss* had at least three symptoms. Only 11 of the 104 did not admit to a major physiological symptom; 8 *Ss* had as many as 11 (median = 4.1 physiological symptoms). All *Ss* had at least two major behavioral and attitudinal indices (median = 3.5). All but one subject had at least one minor behavioral symptom (median = 3.7). We believe on the basis of these data that, no matter what definitional criteria of alcoholism are employed, we had compiled a sample of severe alcoholics.

Not only were these men alcoholic, they had come to the attention of law enforcement institutions. Table 5 indicates their number of arrests. Only 9 had not been in legal trouble. Yet the vast majority of these were misdemeanors; only 17 reported felony arrests. More objective data relating to recent arrests and their type are presented later.

Our sample's mental functioning was judged by their reading ability, IQ, and time taken to complete the Trail Making Test. Reading was determined on a pass-fail basis. According to our modified test, 12 did not

Table 5.   Indicators of alcoholism and legal difficulties

Measure	N	Measures of central tendency
Total amount of ethanol consumed per day when drinking (ounces)		
1–5	13	Mean consumption
6–10	33	(ounces) = 14.9
11–15	26	Median = 11.0
16–20	9	
21–25	9	
26–30	4	
31 or more	10	
Number of total physiological and behavioral symptoms of alcoholism		
3–4	8	Mean number of
5–6	5	symptoms = 11.9
7–8	9	Median = 12.2
9–10	14	Mode = 13.0
11–12	19	
13–14	20	
15–16	14	
17–18	7	
19–21	8	
Number of self-reported lifetime arrests[a]		
0	9	Mean arrests = 28.7
1–2	13	Median = 6.5
3–4	9	Mode = 5.0
5–6	19	
7–8	4	
9–10	7	
11–12	5	
13–15	5	
20–1000	29	

[a] Data not available on 4 Ss.

read at a sixth grade level. Their intelligence was in the low-normal range generally, as Table 6 shows.

One of our major tests for organicity was the Trail Making Test. The cut-offs were supposed to be set at 39 and 91 seconds, respectively, although these were stretched (see Table 6).

It must be remembered that: 1) Ss could be included in the sample if they did not pass one of the tests but did reasonably on the others, and 2) this test is sensitive to alcohol ingestion for several days after it is stopped.

Table 6.   Indicators of intellectual and brain functioning

Measure	N	Measures of central tendency
Kent Scale Measured intelligence (IQ)		
73	3	Mean = 92.5
80	6	Median = 93.3
86	25	Mode = 100
93	32	
100	38	
Time to complete Trail Making Test (in seconds)		
Part A:[a] 0–38	72	
39–44	27	
45–49	0	
50–58	1	
59–65	1	
66–72	2	
Part B:[b] 0–43	3	
44–50	1	
51–56	5	
57–63	7	
64–71	11	
72–78	16	
79–88	18	
89–99	21	
100–145	16	
146 and above	3	

[a] Data not available on 1 subject.
[b] Data not available on 3 Ss.

Table 7 describes our sample in terms of age, education, income, occupational level, social class, and current living arrangement. Only 8 men in our sample had never been married; 61 had been married once, 24 twice, and 8 three or more times. Forty-eight were currently married and only 2 reported no sexual contact.

Thus, as might be expected from our sampling procedures and screening techniques, we ended up with a lower middle class sample of low-normal intelligence alcoholics, having legal troubles but being fairly socially and psychologically adept.

SUCCESS OF RANDOMIZATION

All accepted Ss were randomly assigned to a treatment group. Analyses of variance procedures were performed for the following variables to determine if there were any significant differences between the treatment and control groups: reading, age, education, marital status, present employ-

Table 7.   Sample characteristics for age and socioeconomic indicators

Measure	N	Measures of central tendency
Age range (years)		
24–30	15	Mean age = 39
31–35	27	Median = 38
36–40	16	Mode = 35
41–45	23	
46–50	12	
51–58	11	
Educational level		
Graduated professional	3	Mean years of
College graduate	2	education = 10.4
Partial college	11	Median = 10.7
High school graduate	34	Mode = 12.0
Partial high school	19	
Junior high school	18	
Less than 7 grades of school	17	
Yearly gross income ($)^a		
0–3000	25	
3100–5000	17	
5100–7500	17	
7600–10,000	19	
11,000–15,000	15	
16,000–25,000	4	
above 25,000	1	
Occupational level		
Executive	3	
Manager	3	
Administrator	6	
Clinical	9	
Skilled	31	
Semi-skilled	21	
Unskilled	31	
Hollingshead Social Class Index		
Upper	3	
Upper Middle	3	
Middle	8	
Lower Middle	41	
Lower	49	
Living arrangements at intake		
Alone	19	
Wife	45	
Mother	10	
Both parents	6	
Male roommate	2	
Female roommate	22	

^{a} Data not available on 5 Ss.

Table 8.   Selected intake characteristics of clients initiating treatment

Characteristic	AA[a]	Insight	Lay-RBT[b]	Pro-RBT[c]	Control	Grand mean
Number of clients that initiated treatment	38	38	42	48	31	197
Mean age (years)	39.1	38.3	38.8	41.5	37.9	39.1
Mean years of education	9.2	10.9	10.8	10.2	10.5	10.3
Percent living with wife	36.8	39.5	45.2	39.6	32.3	38.7
Percent unemployed	36.8	21.1	40.5	33.3	25.8	31.5

[a] Alcoholics Anonymous.

[b] Layman-administered rational behavior therapy.

[c] Professionally administered rational behavior therapy.

ment, place of residence, living arrangement, delusions and hallucinations, memory loss, Trail Making Test impairment index (Part A and Part B combined), and the Kent IQ score. No significant differences were found. This indicated that the randomization strategy had been very successful. Table 8 shows this in a breakdown by treatment groups on several key variables.

DROPOUTS vs. COMPLETION ON DRINKING

The Drinking Questionnaire (see Appendix E) was administered at the screening point to select a certain sample. We compared responses of those who dropped out of treatment before 10 sessions with those who completed at least 10 sessions. The results are presented in Appendix P.

Perhaps the overall importance of these data is that so many variables did not discriminate dropouts from those who completed. Such physiological indicators reported as tremors, seizures, delirium tremens ("DTs"), blackouts, loss of control, Trails A and B, age, and the physiological index did not discriminate between these two groups. Likewise behavioral indicators, such as reported trouble on the job or with marriage, alcohol arrests, problems with anger, the major and minor behavioral indices, IQ, education, current employment, mental state, reading, delusions, and hallucinations, did not differentiate between these groups.

However, there were some differences that are at least interesting. Those who stayed with treatment: 1) drank more beer and wine but less liquor than those who dropped out, even though their total consumption of ethanol was similar; 2) tended to be in a slightly "worse shape," i.e., they more often tended to drink for more than 1 day in a row, drank more in the morning, and had more aggregated job, marital, and legal problems; and 3) had severe problems with objective recent memory loss, whereas those without problems or with mild problems tended more to drop out. These indices might provide a data base toward understanding by inference why these men were motivated to stick with treatment.

DIFFERENTIABLE TREATMENTS

Given the highly discrepant philosophies behind RBT, AA, and insight approaches (cf. Chapter 2), one might assume that the treatment techniques would be notably different. Yet since the early study by Fiedler (1950), some have delighted in asserting that all experienced clinicians do the same things in their psychotherapy. We were not willing to put this to an empirical test in the AA group by tape recording their meetings because of the adverse and unpredictable effects that this would have on usual practice. However, we are convinced that these meetings were discriminably different from the other forms of therapy.

Since each professional therapist was asked to tape record each session, we were able to check our two professionally delivered therapies. Fifteen RBT tapes and 15 insight tapes were collected from five insight and four RBT therapists. From this sample, 5 tapes were randomly selected from each group. Thirteen undergraduate students were asked to listen to the first and last 10 minutes of each tape, which were presented to them in random order. Before listening they were given two brief paragraphs describing each type of therapy, and after listening were asked to specify whether the therapy was RBT or insight.

A correlated t test (for dependent groups) revealed that these disinterested observers were highly successful in distinguishing between these therapies ($p < 0.05$):

	Mean of correctly identified tapes	SD
RBT	4.31	0.75
Insight	4.54	0.66

Both treatments were identified with equal ease. As a result of this study we were quite confident that demonstrably different treatments were being applied to our patients.

OUTCOME—POSTTEST DESIGN

Our treatment sample consisted of 104 individuals who were tested on several instruments before and after treatment, as shown in Table 9. Table 10 shows the dependent variables that were analyzed.

Table 9.   Measures employed at each testing interview

| | | Testing interview | | | |
| | | | | | |
Measure	Intake	Outcome	3-month follow up	6-month follow up	9-month follow-up	12-month follow-up
Self-report						
Behavior Rating Scales	*[a]	*	*	*	*	*
Craving questions	*	*	*	*	*	*
Demographics	*	—[a]	—	—	—	—
Personality						
MMPI	*	*	—	—	—	*
Behavioral						
Alcohol vs. money	*	*	*	—	—	*
Arrest record	*	*	—	—	—	*
Finger pain tolerance	*	*	—	*	—	*
Significant other[b]						
Behavior Rating Scales	—	*	—	*	—	—
Additional measure						
therapist evaluation	—	*	—	—	—	—

[a] * indicates measure administered; — indicates measure not administered.

[b] Behavior Rating Scales were completed by an individual who was in frequent interaction with the client.

These variables can be specified operationally by consulting with the appropriate appendix. Depending on the variable, they were analyzed by χ^2 when data were nominal or by one-way analysis of variance (ANOVA) when it could be documented that the assumptions of ordinal data and homogeneity of variance could be met. (Homogeneity of variance was tested by both Cockran's C Test and the Bartlett Box F.) When those assumptions were violated, the nonparametric Kruskal-Wallis ANOVA (K-W) was employed. When significant overall differences were found ($p < 0.05$), a posteriori tests, such as the Student Newman-Keuls (S-N-K), Scheffé, and Mann-Whitney U, were employed.

At intake none of the 74 variables (excluding MMPI) indicated differences between the treatment groups (and control). This is another indication that the random assignment procedure was successful. Thus in this section the groups are compared with regard to outcome results only, i.e., a posttest design. Other ways of approaching the data are considered in turn.

The outcome data show several significant results: a total of 10 for the parametric ANOVA, the same 10 plus 3 more for the K-W, and 4 others by the χ^2 procedure. This is not a great number of results, but many more than expected by chance. All the following results are significant statistically ($p < p.05$).

Days in Treatment—Number of Sessions

There were no differences between the four treatment groups for number of days in treatment; all averaged approximately 210 days. However, the total number of sessions during this time period was different (S-N-K), as Table 11 shows. It appears that layman RBT (lay-RBT) and insight therapy had more sessions per unit time than professional RBT (pro-RBT) and AA. We suspect this is due to the emphasis on relationship factors that occurred in these two types of therapy; perhaps the AA group and pro-RBT were more impersonal or efficient.

Dropouts

Each treatment group was assigned the same number of subjects, and approximately 40 subjects attended at least one session for each group (see Table 8.) However, the Ns reported in Table 11 indicate that AA had significantly less "holding power" than the other treatments.

Economic

There was only one economic variable that differentiated between treatments and control at outcome. Both professionally treated groups were more likely to own a car or be making payments on one as compared to having no economic relationship to a car. Specifically, pro-RBT was significantly better than lay-RBT, AA, and control; insight was significantly better than AA or control by the Mann-Whitney U procedure.

Legal—Self-Report

There were several results where insight therapy generally seemed to be superior:

1. Times picked up by police: lay-RBT and insight therapy better than control.

Table 10.   Basic dependent variable package

Instrument	Number of scored variables
Behavior Rating Scale	
Social	10
Employment	8
Economic	6
Legal	7
Drinking	
Items	13
Created variables	10
Reasons for drinking	14
Craving and Withdrawal Questionnaire	3
Money-alcohol machine	2
Finger Pain Threshold	1
Total	74

Table 11.   Mean number of sessions and number of days in treatment

Group	N	Mean number of sessions	Mean number of days
Pro-RBT	26	19.69	201
Lay-RBT	25	27.64	243
Insight	22	26.09	215
AA	12	20.92	203

2. Times in jail: insight therapy better than AA and control
3. Court appearances: insight therapy and pro-RBT better than control
4. Number of times found guilty: lay-RBT and insight therapy better than control

Mean values were between 1 and 2; differences were found with the nonparametric procedures.

Legal—Police Records

Objective data were obtained on number of arrests for drunkenness, driving while intoxicated, total alcohol-related charges, and total charges. During the year before treatment there were no differences between the five groups, nor were there differences during the year after treatment. However, during treatment there were differences in drunkenness arrests, total alcohol-related charges, and total legal charges. Mean drunkenness arrests are presented as an example of how all three looked: pro-RBT, 1.46; lay RBT, 1.20; insight therapy, 0.41; AA, 1.25; and control, 3.21.

For this particular analysis the Mann-Whitney U Test indicated that all treatment groups were better than no treatment. Depending on the variable, its variance, and the statistical procedure employed, often only the insight group was significantly different than the control group. However, the pattern of means presented for the arrests was similar for all of these comparisons, i.e., treatment groups were better than the control group. This was not a robust result, however, because the mean time between intake and outcome for the control group subjects was 320 days whereas the mean ranged from 201 to 243 days for the treatment groups. Thus this gross, problematic measure was confounded by differing time periods, and no weight can be put on these results.

Social Drinking—Self-Report

For the social drinking self-report variable there was a significant overall F but no a posteriori comparisons of significance, even though the variance was homogeneous. The K-W ANOVA was significant at the 0.06 level and the Mann-Whitney comparisons indicate that drinking to be sociable became relatively more important to the lay-RBT and insight groups than the pro-RBT and control groups. This is a weak result and it would be problematic to venture an interpretation.

AA Group Membership

In the 3 months preceding outcome, patients assigned to the AA treatment group had greater attendance at the AA meetings, as was expected. Whether this would continue during follow-up was doubtful since only 7 of 12 group members considered themselves in AA at outcome and they were not encouraged or coerced to attend. Some patients treated by therapists also attended other AA groups, i.e., at outcome there were four in each of the other treatment groups and three in the control group. However, for each of these groups there was a lesser number with a sponsor—a measure of the intensity of involvement:

2 in pro-RBT
0 in lay-RBT
1 in insight therapy
5 in AA
1 in control

It may be that upon facing termination of other treatment, these men decided to continue with AA as a means of helping themselves further. This level of involvement for a few did not appear to confound follow-up results, even if they continued to attend.

Drinking

For the variable "average number of days dry in the previous 3 months," both insight therapy and pro-RBT did better than the control groups, with an average of 25 more days dry in the period immediately preceding outcome. Lay-RBT and AA were not different from the control group. It was suggested that the insight therapy group did significantly better than the AA group.

For the question "Are you drinking less (in the last 3 months)?" the pattern of responses is significant by χ^2:

Group	Yes	No
Pro-RBT	8	2
Lay-RBT	17	0
Insight	12	1
AA	6	3
Control	5	5

This pattern is repeated for binges and other questions, although these are not different statistically. Again it can be seen that treatment has a positive perceived influence, which does not show up as clearly in the control group. Although this is a weak variable, for this sample at this time, treatment groups have an improvement rate of 88% in comparison to a 50% improvement rate in the control group. Taken in concert with the other drinking variable mentioned above and the direction of the nonsignificant results, there seems to be support for an assertion of decreased drinking for the treated groups.

Therapist Subjective Evaluation

A form was devised for our professional therapists to rate their client's improvement at the end of treatment that paralleled the BRS (see Appendix N). Results on the 19 items were analyzed by K-W one-way ANOVA and χ^2. There were no significant results.

On a post hoc basis it could be said that the categories may be too broad and not behavioral enough, the scoring system not discriminating enough, and the therapists could not be expected to have access to the information needed to make appropriate judgments. In concert this might be expected to produce an "average set" in the responding. However, note that these analyses do not look at changes in the patients—only at differences between the group of therapists' ratings of the two professional groups at outcome. Most therapists rated patients as improved in various ways.

FOLLOW-UP

It is important in every treatment evaluation to examine the permanancy of treatment effects. To assess the impact of time on changes apparently induced by treatment, the Behavior Rating Scales were readministered approximately every 3 months during the year following outcome. Moreover, the entire intake interview was readministered at the 12-month follow-up testing and other measures were administered, as indicated in Table 9. Of the 104 individuals completing outcome, 77.9% (81) completed all four of the follow-up interviews. In addition, 12 individuals who did not take the outcome were tested during follow-up, providing a total of 116 (104 + 12) clients with one or more posttreatment interviews. The number of individuals in each treatment for whom there are posttreatment data is presented in Table 12.

MMPI

We analyzed 126 of the available MMPI scales with regard to the means of the four treatment groups and control during each of three time periods—intake, outcome and 12-month follow-up. There were 15 signifi-

Table 12.   Number of individuals providing follow-up data

Testing completed	AA	Insight	Lay-RBT	Pro-RBT	Control	Total
Outcome and all follow-up	9	19	18	22	13	81
Outcome and some follow-up	3	3	7	4	6	23
No outcome, but some follow-up	2	1	1	3	5	12
Total	14	23	26	29	24	116

cant ($p = 0.05$) results at intake, 9 at outcome, and 8 results at the 12-month follow-up. In view of all the indicators of successful randomization, the relatively small Ns involved for this type of analysis, and the difficulty in making coherent and consistent interpretations of these data, it is probably most parsimonious to regard these as chance findings.

BRS Follow-up

The self-reported behavior of our men on the BRS scale produced 45 variables at the 3-, 6-, 9-, and 12-month follow-up periods. These variables were analyzed by analysis of variance and χ^2. These different ways of approaching the data produced different results. There were more significant results at the 3-month time period for both types of analyses and thereupon a decrement in significant results for each succeeding time period down to only one significant result at 12 months. With the exception of the 3- and 9-month ANOVAs, there was little consistency in the variables that were significant, i.e., in each time period the variables that would differentiate between the treatment groups were different from any other time period. Table 13 summarizes the results that were significant ($p = 0.05$) at each time period by each means of analysis.

The parentheses in Table 13 indicate either an obvious result that was nonsignificant statistically because of large variances or a ratio of the extent to which the means differed from each other. Some of these results are interesting in their own right, but overall it would seem significant that treatment consistently did better than the control in comparisons that were significant. Only a few variables held up consistently in their significance levels and their ranking of groups over time periods, i.e., owning a car, average ounces of alcohol, number of days drinking, average number of times dry at the 3- and 9-month time period. It seems plausible that the variability in these men's behavior (or report) was great during follow-up. However, the pattern is the same when significance is reached on a given variable, and treatment always does better than control despite the changes in dependent variables.

Table 13. BRS significant follow-up results

Method	3 months	6 months	9 months	12 months
ANOVA	Own car, P, I > C Number of days missed work, P > All (ratio 4:1) Number of times stop at 1 or 2 drinks, All treatments > C Overall QFV classification —L, C (All treatments > C—NS) Average ounces alcohol/90 days (All treatments < C) (ratio 1:5) Days drinking/90 days P, L, I < C (ratio 1:2) Average times dry, L, I > C (ratio 2:1)	Employment status, I > AA Number of binges, All groups < AA (ratio 1:4) Drink to work better—AA more important than other groups Drink to feel superior—AA more important than other groups	Average number of drinks per day, P < C (All treatments C—NS) Number of days drinking, P, I < C (All treatments < C—NS) Average number of times dry, P, I > C (L > C—NS)	Total days of drinking, P, I < C (ratio 1:2)
χ^2	P and I own or make payments on car > Others More AA and C live alone Control had more Ss with no days dry/90 days	Employed, I, L best; AA worst Number of times in jail, number of court appearances, I best Employment status (seeking, part, full-time), I best vs. AA and C worst		Been in alcohol treatment center, L; Others < I

Key: P, pro-RBT; L, lay-RBT; I, insight; AA, Alcoholics Anonymous; C, control; NS, not significant.

There is some evidence in the pattern of results at 6 months that the 7 to 10 AA members that were being studied at this point were having considerable trouble. This may not be generalizable because of the small N. Although variable, the AA group's performance overall did seem to be weaker than the other treated groups during follow-up. As follow-up proceeded, the two professional groups seemed to take a superior position at 9 months and provide the only significant results at 12 months. However, of these two professional groups, the insight group had 4 (of 21) members that had been in another alcohol treatment center compared to none (of 23) in the pro-RBT group.

REPEATED MEASURES ANALYSES

BRS

Repeated measured analyses were performed on the basic dependency variable package (see Table 10). All of these variables were analyzed for four time periods—intake, outcome, 3-month, and 12-month follow-up—except for four variables from the Finger Pain Threshold and the Craving and Withdrawal Questionnaire. These latter were analyzed for three time periods—intake, outcome, and 12-month follow-up. This type of analysis can produce two possible main effects, group and time, and one interaction, group by time. Fortunately, we did not get any group effects: This is another comment on our successful randomization procedure. The interaction effect, i.e., groups differentiating over time, would be most desirable, and two of these were obtained that were interpretable. There were also several time effects, i.e., all groups changed over time.

There were no significant interaction effects for any of the treatment groups or the control group except for two in the lay-RBT group. Paired comparisons were done for each of the time periods for each group when a significant interaction effect was found. Two differences were discovered (Table 14) for the item indicating the importance to the person of drinking in order to relax. Table 14 indicates that 3 months after treatment ended it was less important to these men to drink in order to relax. Inspection of the means indicates that this process began (although not significantly) at outcome and continued to its peak at 3 months, but had decreased at the 12-month reading.

In the repeated measures analyses there were five significant results for the main effect of time across all groups (including the control group). Most of these changes took place between intake and the various later time periods. Across all groups there was a decrement in the importance of two self-reported reasons for drinking, i.e., when nervous, and drinking to be cheered up, as Table 15 shows (1 = very important, 3 = not at all important).

Table 14. Repeated measures significant interaction time period comparisons for the lay-RBT group: "I drink to relax"

Times	Mean	SD	Two-tailed t test	df	p
Intake	1.64	0.63			
3 months	2.21	0.80	-2.28	13	0.04
Outcome	1.79	0.89			
3 months	2.21	0.80	-0.12	13	0.054

Table 15 shows that there were changes in the importance of these two reasons for drinking over the time period of treatment. It may be that this is because there was less perceived stress involved at outcome than during the intake period. However, the importance of these reasons continues to decrease during follow-up, so there may be continuing changes occurring on these variables.

Three other main effects for time were noted. The first of these occurred on the self-reported number of times that a man would stop drinking after one or two drinks (1 = never, 5 = abstinent), as Table 16 shows.

The pattern of results indicate that all subjects improved on this variable in the period from intake to outcome, and improvement continued through the 3-month period. At 12 months after treatment these gains had lessened, but were still greater than at the intake period.

The other two time effects are more behavioral, i.e., the number of presses of a button in working for alcohol (in the form of one's favorite beverage) and the number of driving while intoxicated arrests, as shown in Tables 17 and 18.

MMPI Repeated Measures Analyses

Forty variables derived from the MMPI were analyzed by the repeated measures design for the time periods of intake, outcome, and 12 months. In

Table 15. Change in importance of reasons for drinking over time

Reason	Time	Mean	SD	Two-tailed t test Pair	df	t	p
"Need to	Intake	$1.97^{a,b,c}$	0.84	a	65	-1.76	0.08
drink when	3 months	2.32^{b}	0.85	b	65	-2.79	0.007
nervous"	3 months	2.32^{b}	0.79	c	65	-3.33	0.001
($p = 0.016$)	12 months	2.33^{c}	0.75				
"Drinking	Intake	$2.03^{a,b,c}$	0.78	a	65	-1.75	0.085
cheers me up"	Outcome	$2.23^{a,d}$	0.82	b	65	-3.26	0.002
($p = 0.016$)	3 months	$2.39^{b,d}$	0.76	c	65	-3.20	0.002
	12 months	2.36^{c}	0.74	d	65	-1.74	0.086

Identical superscripts indicate which paired comparisons were significantly different.

Table 16. "Number of times stop drinking after 1 or 2 drinks"

Time	Mean	SD	Two-tailed t test			
			Pair	df	t	p
Intake	$2.39^{a,b,c}$	1.26	a	81	-5.23	0.01
Outcome	$3.38^{a,d}$	1.49	b	81	-4.99	0.01
3 months	$3.34^{b,e}$	1.35	c	81	-2.80	0.01
12 months	$2.96^{c,d,e}$	1.43	d	81	-2.12	0.037
			e	81	-2.38	0.020

$p = 0.07$.

Identical superscripts indicate which paired comparisons were significantly different.

these analyses there were three interaction effects and eight time effects, six of the latter being interpretable. (The other two were changes in a correction factor and the Cannot Say score, in the latter case not at a level that would be unexpected for our sample). The five a priori comparisons that were predicted (see p. 53) proved to be nonsignificant in these analyses.

There was a significant ($p = 0.06$) interaction effect on the Hypochondriasis Scale (1) with K correction. Significant paired comparisons are presented in Table 19.

Table 19 indicates that vague somatic complaints and feelings of pessimism decreased significantly in the pro-RBT group during treatment, in the 2 years of treatment and follow-up for the lay-RBT groups, and during follow-up for the insight group.

The second interaction effect ($p = 0.006$) occurred on the Hysteria (3) Scale using original Minnesota norms. Paired comparisons are delineated in Table 20. Again the lay-RBT group decreased during the total time period including treatment and follow-up. The insight group did not decrease during treatment but did during the follow-up period. In contrast, the AA group increased on this variable (which in content is related to somatic complaints and denial of difficulties) all during the process of treatment and follow-up.

Table 17. Number of button presses for alcohol

Time	Mean	SD	Two-tailed t test			
			Pair	df	t	p
Intake	239.4^{a}	348.3	a	41	1.98	0.054
Outcome	$151.2^{a,b}$	204.3	b	41	-2.03	0.049
12 months	221.2^{a}	315.7				

$p = 0.006$.

Identical superscripts indicate which paired comparisons were significantly different.

Table 18.   Number of self-reported driving-while-intoxicated arrests in past 3 months

Time	Mean	SD	Pair	df	t	p
				Two-tailed t test		
Intake	$1.55^{a,b,c}$	0.44	a	65	2.17	0.034
Outcome	1.05^a	0.21	b	65	2.05	0.045
3 months	1.03^b	0.17	c	65	2.60	0.011
12 months	1.02^c	0.12				

$p = 0.003$.

Identical superscripts indicate which paired comparisons were significantly different.

The last interaction ($p = 0.005$) occurred on the Finney Addiction Scale, a variable developed empirically to discriminate narcotic addicts from normals. The paired comparisons are reported in Table 21. On this measure the lay-RBT group increased during treatment (more qualities like people who have trouble with narcotics), the AA group increased during follow-up, and the pro-RBT group decreased in these qualities during treatment and maintained them during follow-up.

Significant comparisons for the time main effects are presented in Table 22. It indicates that our subject pool taken as a whole decreased in psychopathy during treatment. It is possible that this change could be accounted for by the subjects endorsing less items indicating trouble with the legal authorities. In general, anxiety decreased during treatment and stayed down during follow-up, introversion decreased during treatment and stayed down during follow-up, and social desirability increased during treatment. The Holmes and Hampton Alcoholism scales were some of the first developed (cf. Clapton, 1978; Miller, 1976) and indicate a change during the treatment period, which continued. The Hampton scale is thought to measure such qualities as unhappiness, sensitivity, trust, risk taking, and an

Table 19.   Paired comparisons on the Hypochondriasis Scale with K corrections

Group	Mean	SD	t	df	Two-tailed p
Pro-RBT					
Intake	69.7	16.8	1.99	22	0.059
Outcome	63.3	13.15			
Lay-RBT					
Intake	65.6	17.4	3.31	20	0.003
12 months	58.6	18.1			
Insight					
Outcome	61.4	11.3	2.89	20	0.009
12 months	54.7	9.2			

Table 20.   Paired comparisons on the Hysteria Scale

Group	Mean	SD	t	df	Two-tailed p
Lay-RBT					
Intake	66.9	12.4	2.79	20	0.011
12 months	61.3	12.2			
Insight					
Intake	60.0	9.1	2.59	20	0.017
12 months	55.0	8.7			
Outcome	60.1	11.7	2.84	20	0.01
12 months	55.0	8.7			
AA					
Intake	58.1	9.9	−2.54	9	0.032
12 months	66.2	9.5			
Outcome	59.7	5.5	−2.59	9	0.029
12 months	66.2	9.5			

external locus of control. These have been described as scales of general maladjustment and immaturity rather than alcoholism scales per se, even though they were developed empirically to discriminate alcoholics from normals. Thus the thrust of all these changes over time on the MMPI would suggest a better, generalized adjustment, i.e., less anxiety, withdrawal, and troubles generally. Since the control group was not differentiated from the treatment groups in these time analyses, it would appear that these changes would be the result of the initial conditions and their natural changes or development, i.e., in trouble with the law or their families initially and then coping better with their problems over time.

In summary, repeated measures analysis did not yield a great deal of new information but did reveal some trivial findings of interest. The time changes would indicate that these men do change over time, perhaps because of the operation of attention to their problems by an external source and the relatively dysfunctional nature of their lives at the time of intake.

Table 21.   Paired comparisons on Finney Addiction Scale

Group	Mean	SD	t	df	Two-tailed p
Lay-RBT					
Intake	2.1	0.77	−2.91	20	0.009
Outcome	2.6	0.87			
AA					
Outcome	2.2	0.8	−2.71	9	0.024
12 months	2.8	0.9			
Pro-RBT					
Intake	2.4	0.95		22	0.075
Outcome	1.9	0.7			

Table 22. Significant MMPI comparisons of main effects for the time variable

Change over time in	Time period	Mean	SD	df	t	p
Scale 4 (Psychopathy-T corrected) $p = 0.068$)	Intake	5.3	2.8	100	1.91	0.059
	Outcome	4.5	2.7			
Welsh Anxiety Factor ($p = 0.004$)	Intake	52.7	11.2	100	2.75	0.007
	Outcome	49.9	12.5			
	Intake	53.30	11.0	91	3.38	0.001
	12 months	49.7	12.2			
Wiggins Social Desirability Scale ($p = 0.06$)	Intake	49.9	11.3	100	−2.03	0.045
	Outcome	51.8	10.8			
Social Introversion Scale ($p = 0.03$)	Intake	56.3	12.8	91	3.11	0.002
	12 months	53.8	10.9			
Hampton Alcoholism Scale ($p = 0.001$)	Intake	56.8	12.8	100	3.29	0.001
	Outcome	53.5	13.2			
	Intake	57.2	12.9	91	3.66	0.001
	12 months	53.0	12.8			
Holmes Alcoholism Scale ($p = 0.045$)	Intake	60.7	12.1	100	1.74	0.085
	Outcome	58.9	11.1			
	Intake	60.8	11.6	91	2.30	0.024
	12 months	58.8	10.9			

OTHER DEPENDENT MEASURES

The discriminating reader will note the absence in this chapter of a number of dependent measures mentioned in the previous chapters. Because of mechanical breakdowns and inappropriate procedures employed at various times, the data from the Breathalizer and galvanic skin response were judged to be unreliable. They were not analyzed, although they are available on computer disk (requests for data should be addressed to Dr. Brandsma). The finger pain measure was analyzed in the same way as the other measures reported previously, but produced no results. Time, money, and staff constraints precluded doing any predictor analyses at the time. The comparison between the BRS and the BRS-R was not done because of missing data; it was very difficult if not impossible to find a respondent for many of these men, and then to find one that was knowledgeable of their life-style enough to answer the specific questions on drinking pattern, arrests, and financial condition. This was not a good sample of men for testing the validity of this instrument because of the absence of intimate significant others. Any analyses that could have been done would be highly suspect.

RECAPITULATION OF OVERALL STUDY RESULTS

In the interest of completeness and objectivity, all data sources were treated similarly in this chapter; none was focused on excessively. This section not only summarizes major results of the overall comparative study, but heightens those of importance.

Almost half of the largely municipal court subjects screened for our project were not acceptable because of severe deficits in intelligence, reading ability, and organic impairment—usually not psychiatric symptomatology. Of the 260 that were acceptable, only 197 initiated treatment and 104 completed the minimum of at least 10 sessions. These men could be described as lower middle class alcoholics of low-normal intelligence who had significant legal troubles but were fairly socially and psychologically adept. In every instance where intake characteristics were examined, our randomization process proved to be successful in equalizing on important variables across groups.

At outcome, lay-RBT and insight therapy had more sessions per unit time than AA or pro-RBT. AA had the largest dropout rate of any of the treatment groups despite similar social work follow-up. On legal variables the insight group was superior overall, although treatment of any type seemed to help. The two professional treatments seemed to have the most impact on cutting down drinking at the outcome measurement.

When significant differences were found during follow-up, the treated subjects were always superior to the untreated control subjects. The number of significant results decreased over the period of follow-up such that almost no differences between groups were noted at 12 months after treatment ended. With a large number of variables analyzed one would hope to avoid type I errors by showing a consistent pattern, stable over the time period of follow-up. These were the consistent results:

The professionally treated groups were better than the others in owning a car at outcome and 3-month follow-up.

All treated subjects were better than the controls in average ounces of alcohol in the past 90 days at the 3- and 9-month follow-ups.

All treated subjects were better than the controls in the number of days drinking in the past 90 days at the 3- and 9-month follow-ups, with the professional groups being superior to the lay group.

The insight group was superior in the average number of times dry in 90 days at the 3- and 9-month follow-ups.

Over the course of follow-up the professional groups seemed to do better overall and AA the worst overall. MMPI results were complex and difficult to interpret but suggested a generalized adjustment over time for all subjects.

It is noteworthy at this point to put these overall results in the context of a few comparable studies and reviews. Bergin and Lambert (1978) stated after a review of therapy outcome studies that "the largest proportion of variation in therapy outcome is accounted for by pre-existing client factors, such as motivation for change, and the like. Therapist personal factors account for the second largest proportion of change, with technique varia-bles coming in a distant third" (p. 180). Our study has shown some dif-ferences on the basis of technique, but by and large it indicates that minimum treatment of any kind is beneficial, and more so than found in an untreated control group. This is consistent with several other recent reviews of psychotherapy effectiveness. The largest difference in this largely short-term (under 25 sessions) treatment seems to be symptom oriented, i.e., with regard to decreasing drinking and legal problems. We saw no significant superiority for a broad spectrum behavior therapy over a more traditional insight approach, which agrees with Sloane et al. (1975). However, the possible use of this particular behavioral approach in a self-help format may prove to be an advantage for it, especially if supportive follow-up were continued (see Chapter 8).

Although AA plays an extremely important part of a community's response to alcoholism in terms of education and treatment, it seems to have a definite but delimited "place in the sun." This has been documented in several reviews, mentioned earlier. AA seems to have definite limitations of social class, ideology, flexibility of adopting new techniques, and the type of personality it appeals to. Our study suggests further confirmation of this in our severe dropout rate from this form of treatment. It is probable, as Ditman et al.'s (1967) work suggested and ours confirms, that AA is just not effective as a coerced treatment with municipal court offenders.

chapter 5
IMPORTED THERAPISTS: A STRATEGY FOR EXPANDING EFFICIENT ALCOHOLISM SERVICES

The data analyses for the overall comparative study have been completed. However, the study was designed to look at other important questions of interest in the field of alcoholism treatment. Not only did these questions dictate looking at selected subsets of our data, but there was a large amount of variance in our statistical analyses, which could easily be hiding some important effects. Thus, from a data analysis viewpoint, a strategy of selecting similar groups on variables of interest might be successful in reducing variance estimates. Some results from the previous chapter are repeated so that a specific topic can be viewed in its entirety.

Shaw et al. (1978) provide an introduction to our unique use of professionals in this project:

> The nature and extent of the response to a problem is determined by how the problem is perceived and how prevalent it is estimated to be. As we have seen, the immediate post-war years were characterized by a fairly strict disease-model of alcoholism which advocated a specialist response consisting of Alcoholics Anonymous and Psychiatric Alcoholism Services, both primarily aimed at achieving a treatment goal of total abstinence. Gradually concepts of alcohol abuse widened out to perspectives which conceived drinking problems to be much more diverse in nature than the concept of 'alcoholism'. Problems came to be seen as multi-factorial in both cause and effect. Over the same period, studies of both national statistics and general population surveys showed that the prevalence of drinking problems was much more extensive than previously thought. Moreover, much concern was expressed in the 1960s and 70s about the seemingly accelerating growth in the prevalence of alcohol-related problems. These shifts in perspective were not simply challenges to the disease theory, they were also fundamental challenges to the whole rationale of treatment for drinking problems and the ways in which treatment services were organized. Accordingly, there were considerable changes in thinking about the nature and extent of the necessary response (Shaw et al., 1978, p. 105).

Next these authors documented the shift away from specialist inpatient services and their (and AA's) basic inadequacy in coping with the vast number of drinking problems that exist in our society. This shift was not just based on changing ideology or politics—as shifts often are. Instead, there is clear evidence that, on grounds of empirical efficiency, specialist alcoholism services did not do any better than outpatient clinics (in England: Edwards and Guthrie, 1967; Ritson, 1968) or detoxification alone (in America: Stein et al., 1975) no matter how long they were kept in such a unit (Willems, Letemendia, and Arroyable, 1973). Because of these studies and economic factors there has been a shift toward community services: "The shifting stress in policy from hospital to community services accompanied the changing concepts of alcohol abuse away from the idea of alcoholism as a fairly specific disease syndrome to a more comprehensive view of drinking problems as a wide-ranging and varying cluster of social and medical problems" (Shaw et al., 1978, p. 110).

Thus it is documented that community-based (largely outpatient) responses are needed—not necessarily new ones, but ones that better organize community resources. Shaw et al. (1978) continued in their very interesting book to analyze the problems connected with this and proposed a specific solution that is worth reading. In summary, they showed that persons working with alcoholics need motivation, a role identification as a therapist for alcoholics, and available consultation and support. Our importation of therapists from the community seemed to respond to these prerequisites of success. Money provided motivation, the setting provided a role identification and some support, and our training workshop and availability provided a sense that consultation and support were available, even if used infrequently. No matter what the forms of community and specialist organization to confront the problems of alcohol may be in the future, there will always be a need for some professional input as evaluators and counselors.

STRATEGY

Our reasoning was as follows: It has long been recognized that alcoholism programs are often blocked by a lack of both facilities and expertise. Locations that might already contain these necessities, such as a hospital, tend to be overwhelmed with ever-present demands on parking, space, and time. Another problem is that hospital and medical center administrations hesitate to allocate a standard amount of space to alcoholics when there is a shortage of beds (Stein et al., 1975). These hospitals often have busy, impersonal emergency rooms requiring long waiting periods and are not geared to meet the needs of the alcoholic. The alcoholic is perceived as a "special problem" that requires too much attention, is unmotivated, or is not "suitable for treatment in his condition." Consequently, the alcoholic is often refused treatment or is referred elsewhere.

Outpatient programs seem more practical because no one has proved that hospitalization is essential for the treatment of alcoholism (Gerard and Saenger, 1966). Outpatient programs appear to do equally as well as inpatient programs and are perhaps better, in that the outpatient is often able to keep or obtain a job during treatment and remain with his family. Outpatient treatment programs, however, often lack professional expertise. If one wants to adapt the psychological approach to the treatment of alcoholism, one must be prepared to pay at least one full-time, competent professional. Salaries tend to range from $12,000 to $18,000 per year. If the patient load is sizable (more than six patients per day), more than one full-time therapist is required to cope with it. In addition, the therapist frequently acquires numerous clinic or administrative responsibilities, and to compensate the agency must hire additional staff at additional costs.

Two initial problems arose that were crucial to the administration of our research-treatment program. The first was the selection of the location, one that would not be overly crowded or geographically inconvenient. There was no room for the project in the Department of Psychiatry or anywhere else in the medical center. This, combined with our previous unsuccessful experiences with treating alcoholics in the outpatient clinic, prompted us to locate in an office complex off-campus, but on a main street near the center of town, easily accessible by public transportation.

A second problem encountered was: Who would serve as therapists for the project? Rational behavior therapy and insight therapy were to be represented by different therapists; hence it would be essential to acquire the services of at least two professional therapists at the master's or Ph.D. degree level. Intake of patients was scheduled to take place over a period of 2 years, with each patient scheduled for up to 46 weeks of treatment. Thus there would have been a substantial salary outlay if full-time workers had been hired.

Had the project been located at the medical center, professional personnel already present might have been available to the project on a part-time basis. However, we found that only a limited number of specialists in the treatment modalities specified for SHARP desired to work with alcoholics. Furthermore, it was apparent from our previous experiences that alcoholics did not want to come to the hospital for appointments. Instead, we hired professional therapists representing various disciplines (including psychiatry, psychology, and social work) from area hospitals and treatment facilities on a part-time or "moonlighting" basis. Thus the term *imported therapists* emerged.

Many of the therapists worked in the evening, on Saturday, or even on Sunday, depending on the need and/or availability of the alcoholic. This suited the therapists since their jobs kept them busy most of the day. Turnover of professional staff was almost nonexistent probably because the therapists were not confronted with administrative pressures, large caseloads, or multiple agency responsibilities. Instead, they were hired for one specific task, a task in which they had been trained—psychotherapy. In most agencies the therapists must treat a variety of problems and usually have little opportunity to specialize in a particular field of interest. Therapists employed by SHARP, however, expressed a direct interest in working with the alcoholic and having at least a part-time role identification as this kind of specialist. Thus, the factor of self-selection ensured a high level of involvement with alcoholics and their problems. A special workshop was provided for them to be further trained in the specific problems and dynamics of problem drinkers. What evolved was a unique treatment approach consisting solely of part-time professional therapists. The permanent administrative staff of SHARP acted as a liaison between the therapist and the patient.

The imported therapist was paid $25.00 for each therapy session and was directly remunerated only when actual therapy with an alcoholic was conducted. When patients failed to keep scheduled appointments, the therapist was paid a reduced fee ($10.00), and no fee was paid if the patient missed three consecutive appointments. With this type of financial rein-forcement system, therapists were highly motivated to keep their patients in active, outpatient treatment. Thus both the therapist and the patient benefited: the therapist received direct hourly compensation for his services and the alcoholic received increased exposure to treatment.

The imported therapist almost always came to the SHARP office for the therapy session. When the patient did not keep his scheduled appointment, the therapist was responsible for rescheduling. If the patient could not be contacted, the therapist then consulted the project social workers, who in turn conducted rigorous follow-up consisting of telephone calls to the patient himself, family, or relatives. Letters and home visits were other methods that the staff used to get the patient back into treatment.

The therapists seemed to enjoy the informal atmosphere of the project office, which was quite different from the necessarily formal, high-pressure, crowded institutions in which they ordinarily spent their working hours. Relationships between project staff, patients, and therapists were relaxed and friendly.

Cross-fertilization of ideas resulted from therapists seeing the patients in the project office. Although the project research plan called for a comparison of therapeutic modes, each therapist, within the basic framework of either rational behavior therapy or insight therapy, tended to have an individualistic approach. The feeling was that not only patients but staff members and therapists benefited from the exchange of ideas.

RESULTS

By the time the project had been in existence for 30 months, SHARP had used the services of 14 imported therapists. Ten of the 14 continued to function as imported therapists throughout the treatment period. Therapists saw from 1 to 17 patients, with a mean of 6, over the course of the project.

A retention rate of 73% for SHARP patients seen by professional imported therapists was obtained. The criterion for retention in treatment was a stringent one, a minimum of 10 sessions. Patients with less than 10 sessions were regarded as "dropouts."[1] This high retention rate seems significant since it is well-known that dropout rates for patients in regular psychiatric outpatient treatment are high. Hornstra et al. (1972) showed that only 15.2% of their patients made "high" use of outpatient services (more than three appointments kept). This rate confirms the experience of others. In one case, 50% of the patients dropped out of treatment following the first visit (Coleman and Dumas, 1962) and in another case over half of a group of lower socioeconomic level patients randomly assigned to group therapy dropped out within four sessions (Nash, Frank, and Gildeman, 1957).

The dropout rate for alcoholics is even worse. Gerard and Saenger (1966) reported that in a study of seven alcoholism treatment clinics, 52% of the patients came no more than 4 times and 20% came a minimum of 10 times. Kissen, Platz, and Su (1970) found that one-third of the patients in their study (N = 458) dropped out after the initial workup. Ditman and Cohen (1959) reported that in their pharmacologically oriented clinic, 80% of the patients had dropped out of treatment before 1 month. Mendelson and Chafetz (1959) also reported similar findings regarding high dropout rates for alcoholics referred to outpatient treatment. The retention rate acquired by the imported therapists at SHARP, therefore, is significant in comparison to traditional alcoholism programs.

Beyond the recognized importance of retention rates in treatment programs, does therapy result in any measurable changes? Group comparisons of alcoholics treated by imported therapists (pro-RBT and insight) and the control group were done at four time periods: intake, outcome, and 3- and 12-month follow-up. We analyzed 74 variables (see Table 10, Chapter 4); the major instrument used to evaluate the effectiveness of therapy was the Behavior Rating Scale(s). One-way analysis of variance was performed on these variables where appropriate. If overall differences between the three groups proved significant, paired comparisons were done with the Student-Neuman-Keuls procedure. On dichotomous variables χ^2 was employed.

---

[1] Our retention study considered only those patients who had at least one therapy session. Treatment was defined as having had at least 10 sessions or more. Dropout was defined as at least 1 but not as many as 10 therapy sessions. (Persons admitted to the program who never appeared for a first therapy session were not included in the retention study. The group who failed to appear for a first therapy session constituted 25% of those who passed the initial screening.)

INTAKE

At intake there were four significant results—about what would be expected statistically by chance. However, because these results might bias outcome or follow-up results, they are reported here. The control group paid significantly (p = 0.0001) more per month for housing. The insight group was more likely (p = 0.02) than the control to be living with someone (only 1 of 22 lived alone vs. 8 of 19 for the control). At intake, seven of the pro-RBT group and four of the insight group said they were currently in AA; this contrasted (for the pro-RBT group at the 0.05 level) with none in the control group. On whether the patient had had any dry days, three of the control group answered negatively whereas none of the therapy group patients did (p = 0.02). These results are commented upon where they re-occur in the other analyses.

OUTCOME

At outcome there were the following statistically significant terms: one economic variable, four legal variables, three behavioral indicators, and five other variables concerned with drinking. Both the pro-RBT and insight groups were doing better economically: more of them owned a car. Table 23 shows more specifically how this was broken down.

The four legal variables were very similar in means and significance level (p = 0.02), as indeed they are highly interdependent. On the number of times picked up by police (with means between 1 and 2), both the treatment groups were better than the control. The pattern was similar for number of times in jail, number of court appearances, and number of times guilty, except that only the insight group was significantly different from the control in a posteriori comparisons on these latter three variables.

At outcome we recorded three behavioral differences, two involving working for money and alcohol (Table 24). The third behavioral difference concerned getting into specialist inpatient treatment units. Fewer members of treatment groups had been in an alcohol treatment center (p = 0.03); none from the pro-RBT and only one from insight therapy had been in specialist treatment centers, as compared to four in the control group.

In a posteriori analysis only the pro-RBT group score was significantly lower than the control on the money variable, but both treatment groups

Table 23.   Car ownership

| Stage of ownership | Number of subjects | | |
	Pro-RBT	Insight	Control
None	6	7	13
Making payments	5	5	1
Own a car	14	10	5

Table 24.   Mean total button presses for money and alcohol

Group	Money ($p = 0.05$)	Alcohol ($p = 0.02$)
Pro-RBT	217.0	87.4
Insight	327.4	107.2
Control	526.0	316.4

were better than the control in working for alcohol. In inspecting the data we found that the control group worked harder for both money and alcohol—about twice as hard as the treatment groups for money and three times as hard for alcohol. These results are hard to interpret, but perhaps the control subjects were less desensitized to our treatment and testing situation and were more motivated to perform on this particular task involving money. However, this hypothesis cannot account for the proportionately (compared to itself) higher work output for alcohol.

The other outcome results concern drinking. On whether one was drinking less, as mentioned in the overall comparisons, the level of significance was marginal ($p = 0.06$) and there were no a posteriori comparisons reaching significance. However, the table of results is telling (Table 25). The control group had the kind of response one would have expected from an untreated group, whereas the treatment groups were almost twice as likely to say yes.

A similar pattern was evident on the question of having had any dry days in the last 3 months ($p = 0.04$). Exactly as at intake, none of the treated patients said no, but three of the control group did. Because of the preexisting difference, this cannot be given any weight. However, clearer results are forthcoming on the other drinking variables that are more specific.

On the reported number of times that a person had stopped after one or two drinks in the past 90 days, both of the treated groups were superior to the control ($p = 0.04$). The total number of days drinking was even more striking ($p = 0.02$): pro-RBT reported 19.2 days; insight therapy, 18.4 days; and control, 43.1 days.

The converse of this variable, computed by multiplying the number of times dry and the average number of days dry to get the average days dry in the past 90 days, showed an exactly complementary pattern at the 0.005 level, as would be expected.

Table 25.   Have you been drinking less in the last 3 months?

Response	Pro-RBT	Insight therapy	Control
Yes	8	12	5
No	2	1	5

THREE-MONTH FOLLOW-UP

At 3 months after treatment the living with someone proportional break-down was essentially the same as at intake. The same was true for the question on any days dry. The control group was more likely to miss a meal than the treated groups (p = 0.04). The treated groups maintained their superiority on the number of times they had stopped after one or two drinks (p = 0.02). Four members of the pro-RBT group admitted to abusing other kinds of drugs, whereas none in the other groups did. Finally, the control group indicated (p = 0.02) that it was significantly more important for them to drink in order to cheer up.

TWELVE-MONTH FOLLOW-UP

There were only two results at this point in follow-up. The living with someone pattern was repeated in the same proportions as at intake. More important, the total number of days drinking was almost exactly the same as at outcome, with the treated groups better than the control (p = 0.007).

DISCUSSION

Overall, both treatments seemed about equally beneficial when compared to the control. The major lasting impact seemed to be in helping these men cut down on and control their drinking, although other effects were also noted. Treatment effects seemed most notable at outcome, and then trailed off as follow-up proceeded. This fact emphasizes the need for some form of therapeutic follow-up (perhaps self-help groups) over the long term.

Another aspect of this approach is cost effectiveness. Over a 2-year period our imported therapists delivered 1423 interviews at a cost of slightly more than $35,575.00 (more because of our missed interview policy). This compares very favorably with the cost of hiring an extra staff member, who usually only gives 30%–40% of his time to direct service (15 interviews per week at a $16,000 salary). Costs of office space would be the same in either case. Although direct comparisons to other programs are difficult, we do know that our therapists were largely successful and saved the community a lot of money (see Chapter 6). Likewise we believe that our strategy would do a better job in terms of therapist "burn out," and this would be reflected eventually in the success rate.

What, then, are the virtues of the imported therapists approach? First, outpatient services can be advantageously located away from the crowded and unreceptive hospitals and still obtain top-level expertise. Second, importing therapists is similar in price to paying permanent staff members and saves the community a great deal of money. Third, the employment of part-time, highly trained therapists has resulted in increased patient attendance rates and a reduction of drinking behaviors. Fourth, the operation of a flexible treatment program allows for alcoholic patients with jobs to be accommodated in the evening and even on weekends. Fifth, a variety of specialized therapeutic approaches can be gathered together, bringing cross-fertilization of ideas and methods from various localities. Last, but yet perhaps most important, is the philosophical but yet very practical issue of therapist identity as a specialist. Specialization, along with self-selection, can and often does result in a more competent and motivated therapist who treats clients of their own choosing as opposed to those whom the agency dictates must be treated.

chapter 6
THE EFFICACY OF COERCION

The employment of various coercive pressures from the court system has a long history in this and other countries (Chafetz, 1962, 1965). Claims of effectiveness are common, but the empirical studies are decidedly mixed. As an example, Gallant et al. (1973) were initially encouraged by their success with criminal parolees, but later with municipal court offenders and a better designed study they obtained terrible results with all groups when they compared voluntary outpatient treatment to both compulsory inpatient/outpatient and compulsory outpatient treatment. Only 17 of 210 patients were able to be followed up, and the number for each group was too small to base conclusions on. In the literature, at least, interest seems to have waned since then. Baekeland et al. (1975) suggested in conclusion that coercion is probably useful with lower socioeconomic status persons (skid row) if the persons are carefully selected. This brief exposure does not begin to iterate all the reports, but it is obvious that more data are needed to decipher the important distinctions in this area of alcoholism treatment.

Without doubt the costs to society of the "revolving door alcoholic" are enormous. Lexington has between 30 and 50 arrests of drunkenness offenders per day. Gallant et al. (1973) estimated that each of these arrests took between 2 and 4 hours of police time and cost the city $130.000 per arrest in 1967 dollars; that figure could be safely doubled today. He also estimated that 60% to 75% of prisoners in jail were there because of problems relating to alcohol. That was in New Orleans, but the extent of the problem is similar in most cities.

There are some ethical problems involved when a society purports to guarantee civil liberties and the rights of the individual. Yet the person who abuses alcohol usually comes under severe coercive pressures from aversive consequences. These pressures may be applied by the self, the spouse, relatives, employer, physician, or the legal system as a last resort. The more irresponsibly the person behaves, the more social constraints are put on his degree of choice.

METHODOLOGY

In carrying out our long-term research project a reliable group of patients was needed to give our treatments and hypotheses a reasonable test. After resistance from industry we turned to the courts as our major source of referrals. By historical accident we came to have two groups of coerced patients—those referred by the "old" court system (before merger of the city and county governments) and those referred by the "new" court system.

While the government was reorganizing, our project was developing more efficient procedures for keeping these men in treatment.

The old court system was informal and had offenders who were sent to us sign an authorization form similar to that found in Appendix A. The "new" court system became better organized, more formal, and added a detention service and form of legal probation, while we in conjunction had developed better forms (see Appendices B and C) and a working relationship with the courts (see Chapter 2). Briefly, if an offender decided on treatment rather than jail, our project social worker was made his parole officer. If he did not continue treatment for 1 year or until his therapist thought he had completed therapy, the judge would be informed and could reimpose a 30-day jail sentence. It is our perception that: 1) alcoholics always chose treatment rather than jail and 2) only infrequently did the judge revoke probation and impose sentence. In most cases the social worker-parole officer could cajole the person back into treatment (at least for 10 sessions) simply by threatening to report back to the judge.

Our project had two other groups of interest in this regard. First, the voluntary self-referrals were under no legal coercion to attend. Second, the control group was under legal scrutiny (i.e., had no volunteers in it) and "coerced," but received no treatment from us. These four groups, then, can be conceived to constitute a continuum of legal coercion anchored by the volunteers at one end and the new court referrals at the other. Since a case could be made that the separate treatment group effects were relatively similar, it would seem legitimate to collapse treatments and look at the effects of coercion upon outcome in terms of objective arrests, attendance, and BRS performance.

RESULTS

The number of subjects involved in the following analyses depends on whether the person had one or more but not as many as 10 sessions (a dropout) for the dropout data and those that had 10 or more sessions for the other analyses. In the case of the control group, 31 were acquired at intake but only 19 were left at outcome. Table 26 shows the specific numbers of subjects per group.

Analysis of variance was employed to search for overall difference between the groups and the paired comparisons were done with the Student Neuman-Keuls procedure. Chi square was also employed where appropriate.

Dropouts

We used χ^2 to examine the percentage of dropouts and their reasons for dropping out to see if any patterns could be discerned. Table 27 indicates

Table 26.   Number of subjects in various coercion analyses

Subject	New court	Old court	Volunteer	Control
Dropouts	62	63	56	31 (intake)
Completors	37	19	29	19 (outcome)

the percentage of dropout for each group (from the total sample of 257), with the numbers of subjects involved indicated in parentheses. Chi square analysis for Table 27 was highly significant ($\chi^2 = 25.7$; df $= 3$, $p < 0.001$). The pattern indicates that the old court had a greater percentage of dropouts from treatment, approximately twice as many as the other two groups.

The reasons for dropping out are indicated in Table 28, with the percentage of Ss and N indicated as in Table 27. Chi square indicated significant difference between these categories ($\chi^2 = 47.6$; df $= 24$; $p < 0.003$). By inspection it seems obvious that a greater percentage of the new court and volunteers remained in treatment. In complement to this, a greater percentage of the old court moved away or refused to continue. As would be expected, a greater percentage of the new court subjects had their probation revoked. A large number of volunteers refused to continue treatment.

Attendance

Those Ss who were retained for at least 10 sessions were interviewed at outcome and their therapist's attendance records were collected. At outcome our three groups were compared to the 19 control Ss, and it was found that these four groups were no different in the number of other types of alcoholism treatments they had sought in the community on their own. Indeed, the means were minuscule (0.03–0.32) for all of these groups, with the control and old court slightly more. A variable was created from the therapist records called "percent treatments attended" by dividing the number of assigned treatments by the number of assigned plus the number of missed treatments. The means were all between 90% and 92%, with differences being nonsignificant. However, there is a good chance of bias in the data because our payment policy may have decreased the therapists' moti-

Table 27.   Percentage of dropout for all accepted clients ($N = 257$)

Subject	New court	Old court	Volunteer	Control
Dropouts	9.7 (25)	23.7 (61)	12.8 (33)	7.4 (19)
Completors	17.9 (46)	7.8 (20)	13.2 (34)	7.4 (19)

The numbers of subjects involved are indicated in parentheses.

Table 28.   Percentage of dropout for various reasons for all accepted clients (N = 257)

Reason	New	Old	Volunteer	Control
Unknown	1.6 (4)	1.9 (5)	0.8 (2)	0.4 (1)
Deceased	0.8 (2)	0.4 (2)	1.2 (3)	0.0 (0)
Hospitalized	0.8 (2)	0.8 (2)	0.8 (2)	0.4 (1)
Prison	0.8 (2)	0.8 (2)	0.0 (0)	0.4 (1)
Moved	5.4 (14)	8.2 (21)	5.1 (13)	5.1 (13)
Refused to continue	1.2 (3)	10.5 (27)	6.6 (17)	1.2 (3)
Released from probation	0.4 (1)	0.8 (2)	0.0 (0)	0.0 (0)
Probation revoked	3.1 (8)	1.2 (3)	1.2 (3)	0.0 (0)
Completor	13.5 (35)	7.0 (18)	10.5 (27)	7.4 (19)

The numbers of subjects involved are indicated in parentheses.

vation to record misses accurately after three sessions had been missed. This possibility is supported in the data that follow.

The mean number of treatments and days in treatment (more reliable data) are reported in Table 29. The difference in days did not reach an acceptable level of significance (p = 0.10), but the difference between the number of sessions did (p = 0.04). Beyond inspection, a posteriori analyses confirmed that the old court's number of treatments was less than those of the new court or volunteers, who were similar to each other. Thus Table 29 strongly suggests that the old court subjects missed more appointments. The average patient from the old court system kept a mean of 20 appointments in 35 weeks; assuming that the usual appointment frequency was once per week, he missed as many as he kept.

Objective Arrest Records

Analysis of variance was performed on the four groups (N = 104) with regard to their objective arrest data for the year before treatment, the time during treatment, and the year after treatment. The time during treatment was not the same for each group, as is reported in Table 29. There were no

Table 29.   Mean number of treatments attended and days in treatment

Group	Treatments	Days
Old court	20.0	246
New court	25.3	202
Volunteer	24.5	219
Control	none	320

differences between groups in driving while intoxicated charges in any time period. There were no differences between groups in total nonalcohol-related charges during the year before or year after, but during treatment the old court group had more charges than any of the other three groups ($p = 0.08$) (means were between 0.2 and 1.2). When considering that their time in treatment (see Table 30) was longer, it is most reasonable to dismiss this trend. In the year before treatment the disorderly conduct charges were greater for the old court group in comparison to the volunteers; this difference disappeared for the time during and the year after.

There were preexisting significant differences during the year before treatment in the following manner:

Drunkenness	Old > New; Old > Volunteers
Total alcohol-related charges	Old > New; Old > Volunteers
Total charges	Old > New; Old > Volunteers; Old > Control

Here is some evidence that the old court subjects were more delinquent than the subjects in the other groups. This may be because the old court was first in time, and the judges may have dumped their most troublesome cases on SHARP initially. These differences were maintained for the time during treatment and the year after and thus are not related to treatment. However, there were significant differences found between groups in number of drunkenness-arrests during treatment. Both the new court group and the volunteers had fewer drunkenness arrests than the control group. Again this could have been a function of these groups having approximately one-third less time than the control. However, this difference was continued strongly ($p < 0.0001$) during the year of follow-up wherein the time was equalized for each group. Table 31 may be instructive in this regard. Identical superscripts indicate a significant difference between these groups, at least at the 0.05 level. Thus the change in drunkenness arrests seems robust for those that stayed with treatment because of internal motivation (volunteers) or external motivation (new court parolees).

Table 30. Mean and standard deviation of drunkenness arrests for the year following treatment

Group	Mean	SD
New court	$0.84^{a,b}$	1.85
Old court	$5.53^{a,c}$	6.12
Volunteers	$0.93^{c,d}$	1.75
Control	$4.00^{b,d}$	6.64

Identical superscripts indicate a significant difference between the groups so identified ($p = 0.05$).

Table 31.   Average number of days drinking and drinks
per day at outcome

Group	Number of days	Number of drinks
New court	20.1[a]	1.7[a]
Old court	26.5	6.2
Volunteers	23.3	4.6
Control	43.1[a]	11.1[a]

Identical superscripts indicate a significant difference between
the groups so identified ($p = 0.05$).

The BRS scales were also analyzed for our four coercion groups. The differences at intake are what would be expected on the basis of selection, i.e., the volunteers were very different from the other groups in the number of times picked up, court appearances, number of times guilty, and number of times in jail. Beyond this there was evidence that the volunteers had been looking for help, i.e., they had attended more AA meetings at a mean rate of one in the past 3 months.

At outcome the BRS indicated differences in one legal variable and several drinking variables. As mentioned before, at intake the volunteers were less likely to have been picked up by the police; at outcome the new court subjects had joined them in having been significantly fewer times picked up ($p = 0.0001$) than the old court and control subjects. On the drinking variables the new court reported being dry two to three times more often ($p = 0.008$) than the others. For the number of times they had stopped after one or two drinks ($p = 0.03$), the new court, old court, and volunteers were similar and reported significantly more occasions than the control group. The means for number of days drinking in the past 90 days ($p = 0.06$) and average number of drinks per day when drinking ($p = 0.03$) are reported in Table 31.

In terms of a posteriori comparisons, the superscripts indicate that only the new court was significantly different than the control, although all the treated groups did better than the control. Table 31 shows the clinical significance of coercion, a large drop in number of days drinking, and the amount drunk when drinking.

Chi square analyses backed up these results. More subjects in the treated groups said they were drinking less at outcome than did controls. There was also evidence that more of the old court group had joined AA at outcome and had acquired a sponsor, from three members at intake to seven at outcome, whereas there were no changes in the other groups.

DISCUSSION

In these analyses it becomes clear that effective coercion seemed to have positive effects on the outcome of the new court parolees, generally showing them to do as well as volunteers (self-motivated), and in some ways better. Not only did they attend treatment at a higher rate per unit time, but they reported doing better at outcome and were backed up in this regard by objective arrest data.

Our data (Table 28) indicated that probation was only revoked for eight of our subjects in the new court system. Although eight is not many, it seems that word travels fast in this population. With our more formal and effective court procedures in conjunction with the judge's cooperation (including revocation of probation and imposition of sentence), treatment attendance was seen as "serious business," something that could not lightly be ignored. This reputation probably had a lot to do with the effectiveness of our social work follow-up. Only 3 members of the new court group flatly refused to continue, whereas 27 of the old court had done so.

Although other interpretations could be offered, it seems to us that in comparison to previous studies ours did better because of the role of the social worker-parole officer. This person provided a tangible evidence of "the long arm of the law" in finding wayward patients and cajoling them back into treatment. The role was largely persuasive and not immediately punitive, although the threat of a 30-day jail sentence was enough encouragement for a man to honor his written commitment. This person also provided close liaison with the courts in terms of authorization forms (and explanation), referral problems, and, when necessary, the passing of a sentence. This melding of professions seems appropriate in dealing with a population of revolving door alcoholics, and provides a model of treatment that might profitably be employed in any large community. We suspect that the personal touch and continued reminders (backed up by a reputation of really imposing sentences) make for more consistent attendance in treatment; treatment of a minimum amount (5–10 sessions) seems to cut down on drinking and thus on legal troubles.

A rough cost-benefit analysis of this program will shed some further light on these data. In the case of arrests, small mean differences have very large social and economic ramifications for our communities. We consulted with our police department and the court system to get an estimate of costs per arrest. A recent Weighted Caseload Study (Final Report, 1976) was helpful in estimating judicial and nonjudical costs. Estimated dollar costs per arrest in 1978 were: police salary (two officers) and vehicle, $180.00; nonjudicial court costs, $27.50; average judicial cost, $5.00; jail at $25.00 for 2 days, $50.00; for a total of $262.50. These estimations include the following assumptions:

Judge's salary at $25,500 for 215 working days per year and 4.75 hours on the bench per working day

Nonjudicial personnel at an average of $1000 per month, 6.5 hours of work relevant to arrests per day

Most drinking-related arrests occur at night and require two officers per patrol car

Estimations do not include costs of buildings, maintenance, supplies for the courts or jail, nor the salary costs of the staff in jail

Using the $262.50 figure as a rough estimate (perhaps conservative compared to larger cities) and looking at the self-reported variable "Times picked up in the last 3 months" at outcome, there is an average difference between the means of the new court as compared to the old court and control of 0.6 arrest per man. Considering that there were 37 men in the new court group only, this is 23 less arrests in a 3-month period. At $262.50 and with 2 hours of police time per arrest, this is a savings of $6,037 in 3 months ($24,100 projected per year) in direct costs to the community and 8 hours of police time per week.

If we examine the objective drunkenness arrests in the year after treatment (see Table 30) with the same assumptions, we find conservatively an average of 3.1 less arrests per man (i.e., the effective coercion group (new court) compared to the Control). This comes to 115 fewer arrests per year or direct savings to the community of $30,197 and 10 hours of police time per week.

Thus on one measure for only one treated group we have a direct savings of up to $24,100 projected per year during treatment and on the other $30,187 confirmed during a year of follow-up. There is obviously a great savings when these two year figures for 37 subjects are summed and compared to the cost over 4 years of $35,575 as reported for the imported professional therapists to treat 48 subjects. It should be noted and emphasized beyond this that effective alcoholism treatment is cost-beneficial to the community, not only in direct expenses and police time, but in human costs as well.

chapter 7
SELF-HELP METHODS

In this chapter we compare our two self-help methods to each other and to the control. No matter whose statistics or estimates one believes to be accurate, there is a tremendous gulf between the number of persons with alcohol problems and the amount of treatment delivered. Perhaps in the next decade social attitudes toward alcohol may allow more alcoholics to seek help. Since existing treatments can perhaps handle 20% of these problems, there is obviously a great need for alternative intervention strategies that are effective and efficient.

Ours was the first prospective study of AA's effectiveness. Our intent was not to diminish AA in any way, but to evaluate the limits of its effectiveness and perhaps contribute to its betterment (cf. Brandsma, 1976). In addition, it is likely that AA is not everybody's "cup of tea" (Baekeland et al., 1975; Emrick et al., 1977), and other methods must be available if one or several fail.

In this chapter, as in the next, three of the five original groups are analyzed at four time periods—intake, outcome, 3-month follow-up, and 12-month follow-up. These three groups were chosen out of the larger research project mainly because of the important empirical questions that would be addressed. Beyond this, the greater similarity of these groups might have decreased the variance problems encountered in statistical analysis of all five groups.

Methodological descriptions of the "therapists," groups, and measures employed appear earlier in this book. One-way ANOVA was performed on 74 variables (see Table 10, Chapter 4). If overall differences between the three groups proved significant, paired comparisons of the groups were done with the Student Neuman-Keuls procedure. On dichotomous variables (yes/no), χ^2 was employed.

RESULTS

At intake there were two significant ($p < 0.05$) differences found between the two treatment groups. It was more important to drink in order to relax for the lay-RBT group. Second, the AA group reported an average of 1.92 days of missed work in the last 3 months as compared to the 4.24 average for the lay-RBT group. With only 2 of 70 variables being significant, there is a high probability that these results are due to chance factors. This interpretation is strengthened by the variables not proving significant at outcome. Thus these differences at intake do not seem to be biasing the outcome results.

The variables that showed significant differences at outcome could be organized into three categories: treatment holding power, legal difficulties, and drinking behavior. Treatment holding power was indicated by the percentage of dropouts between intake and outcome (p = 0.05), the mean number of treatment sessions attended (p = 0.05), and the mean number of days in treatment. Less than one-third (31.6%) of the clients assigned to the AA group qualified for outcome measures in contrast to almost 60% for the lay-RBT group, and this occurred with equivalent attempts by our social work staff to keep the men in treatment, whatever type it was. Table 32 highlights these differences.

There were two measures of legal difficulties, both self-reported during the last 3 months. The means for the number of arrests (p = 0.04) are: lay-RBT, 1.24; AA, 1.67; and control, 1.79. The results for convictions (p = 0.02) are very similar.

The lay-RBT group had significantly fewer arrests and convictions than did the control group. The AA group was not differentiated from the other two upon a posteriori analysis, but it is clear that the pattern of means favored the lay-RBT group.

At outcome there were no significant differences in drinking behavior between the three groups with regard to the number reporting abstinence. However, the treated groups reported a significantly smaller number of drinks (of beer, wine, and liquor summated) (p = 0.04) per day when drinking, and fewer mean ounces of alcohol (p = 0.06) than the control group. Table 33 indicates that the two treatment groups were similar on both measures of drinking, and that these means were three to four times less than those of the control group.

On the variable indicating how many times the patient had stopped after one or two drinks, the overall analysis was significant (p = 0.03), but the a posteriori comparisons were not. However, the pattern of means showed both treatment groups to have stopped more often than the control (Control = 2.4, lay-RBT = 3.5, AA = 3.7).

All of the lay-RBT clients reported drinking less during the last 3 months. This was significantly better than the AA or the control groups at the 0.005 level. The lay-RBT group also reported on two variables (one a direct question, the other a summated series of questions) that it was less important to drink now to be sociable. In this regard the lay-RBT group

Table 32.   Mean number of treatment sessions and days in treatment

Group	N at intake	N at outcome	Mean number of sessions	Mean number of days treated
AA	38	12	20.9	203
Lay-RBT	42	25	27.6	243

Table 33.   Total daily intake of alcohol when drinking

Group	Mean number of alcoholic drinks per day when drinking	Mean number of ounces of alcohol when drinking
AA	2.47	1.19
Lay-RBT	3.21	1.66
Control	11.16	5.34

was significantly different from the control group, whereas the AA group was not differentiated from either of the other two groups.

Three months after terminating treatment the only variables that revealed differences concerned drinking behavior. The treatment groups maintained their superiority over the control (p = 0.002) in the number of times they stopped drinking after one or two drinks (almost twice as often). The mean number of reported binges was signficantly greater (p = 0.04) for the AA group (2.37 in past 3 months) in contrast to both the control (0.56) and lay-RBT group (0.26). In this analysis AA was five times more likely to binge than the control and nine times more likely than the lay-RBT. The AA group average was 2.4 binges in the last 3 months since outcome.

It was more important at the 3-month follow-up for the control group to drink in order to relax and least important for the lay-RBT group (p = 0.01). This was a complete reversal from the lay-RBT group's attitude at intake. Likewise it was significantly (p = 0.06) less important for the lay-RBT group to drink in order to be cheered up—especially when compared to the control group. A few members of the AA group admitted that drinking made them feel superior (p = 0.01). This pulled their mean score away from the lay-RBT and control groups significantly because none of these latter patients said that this was an important reason for drinking to them.

There were no significant results to report at 12-month follow-up. In certain cases where the data were inspected, part of the reason for this seemed to be the improvement of the control group.

DISCUSSION

In general, it seems again that treatment has beneficial, if short-term, effects in contrast to no treatment. The superior holding power of the lay-RBT method with this population is a definite advantage for it. As Armor et al. (1978) have noted, "the single most important factor that consistently determines improvement is the amount of treatment. The greater the amount of treatment, the greater is the improvement rate." In this sense lay-RBT was definitely superior to the AA group in our study and goes along with the suggestion from the Ditman et al. (1967) study that compulsory AA does not work well with municipal court offenders. At the very least it would seem to be a reasonable alternative for those alcoholics who refuse AA or do not seem to benefit by it.

The 3-month follow-up indicated that AA members had increased their binges and more often drank in order to feel superior. Perhaps the philosophy of total abstinence did not work well for these men—perhaps it led to depression and a tendency to go from one extreme to the other. This is admittedly speculative, but it adds a qualification to Emrick et al.'s (1977) suggestion that AA is more effective than professionals with regard to abstinence.

The lack of results at 12-month follow-up points to a need for continuing support of these men even after "active treatment" has stopped. These men seem to need over an extended period of time not only the structure and support of specific, self-help, problem-solving methods, but the reinforcing effects of a group or individual supportive relationship (cf. Pattison, Sobell, and Sobell, 1977). It would seem that alcohol dependency must be replaced with interpersonal dependency, which will then gradually be resolved in the direction of a more adaptive autonomy.

chapter 8
PROFESSIONAL VS. NONPROFESSIONAL TREATMENT

In keeping with our strategy of reducing statistical variance problems by looking at subsets of our treatment groups, and also to shed some light on important therapeutic issues, we compared the professionally delivered rational therapy to the layman-administered treatment, and both of these against the control. A few words of introduction may serve to highlight the practical importance of this subject.

Within the last decade, individuals, institutions, and federal programs have made increasing demands on mental health professionals for their services. As a consequence of these demands, individuals without formal professional education have been enlisted, trained, and relied upon to function as primary therapists. Thus teachers, parents, peers, and college students are among the individuals who have been successfully trained to implement behavior therapy with children, provide companionship therapy for adolescents and elderly adults, or to serve as counselors in institutions and social action programs. (For specific studies in each of these areas and a review, see Guerney, 1969.)

Programs designed to treat alcoholics have also made frequent use of nonprofessional helping agents (Root, 1973). Moreover, considerable attention has been directed toward the training and evaluating the effectiveness of these alcoholism workers (Cooke, Wehmer, and Gruber, 1975; Rosenberg et al., 1976; Staub and Kent, 1973).

In general the response toward using nonprofessional therapists has been enthusiastic. Not only do they provide needed manpower and thus increase program contact, but they provide additional benefits as well. Guerney (1969) noted that when the helping agent is a significant other, there is an emotional bond that professional therapists could rarely obtain, and this bond seems to aid rather than impede the therapeutic process. A second benefit is client contact; nonprofessional agents are likely to spend more time with the client than professionals could afford. Finally, the helping agent may be more similar to the client than the professional; thus nonprofessionals may understand client problems more readily (Zax and

---

The authors are deeply indebted to Dennis McCarty and Robert Wetter, who collaborated in an earlier draft of this chapter, a paper presented at the Society for Psychotherapy Research, Madison, Wisconsin, June, 1977.

Cowen, 1976). Unfortunately, there is little direct evidence to support this supposition.

Karlsruher (1974) reviewed studies that examined the functioning of nonprofessional therapists. The evidence suggested that nonprofessionals can affect positive change in inpatient and outpatient adults. However, only 1 of these 18 studies included professional therapists, nonprofessional therapists, and no-treatment controls. Without each of these three groups it is not likely that the differential effectiveness of professional and non-professional therapists can be assessed adequately. Karlsruher also noted additional problems in these studies of nonprofessional therapists. The terms *professional* and *nonprofessional* are not clearly defined; thus their meaning may vary from study to study. He suggested that the training and experience of each therapist be clearly stated. Similarly, the type of treatment used by professionals and nonprofessionals was not always the same. Therefore even when both groups were included in the same study, client changes could be a function of therapy rather than level of therapist. As a result of these and other deficiencies, Karlsruher concluded that additional studies are needed (cf. Anthony and Carkhuff, 1977, for a more recent overview).

The present investigation is of interest because comparisons between clients with either professional psychotherapists, nonprofessional psychotherapist, or no psychotherapist can be made. Moreover, the comparisons can be limited to professional and nonprofessional psychotherapists who received similar training and attempted to implement the same type of psychotherapy. In view of this deficit in the literature, such comparisons may be valuable in assessing the general worth of nonprofessional therapists and their effectiveness relative to professional therapists.

Since all indications reported earlier supported the hypothesis of no differences between the groups at intake (because of random assignment), we thought these comparisons would be legitimate. Descriptions of the groups, therapists, and measures appear earlier in the book. For this study 74 variables were analyzed. These included 12 MMPI scales, which were nonsignificant or uninterpretable, and the objective arrest record. The main dependent variables come from the BRS.

One factor that was not random or equalized was the amount of time during treatment. The control group data were collected on an average of 320 days after intake. In contrast the treatment groups averaged 243 (lay) and 201 (professional) in treatment. This lesser amount of time may account for the arrest results that are reported.

RESULTS

One-way analysis of variance was performed on these variables where appropriate. If overall differences proved significant, paired comparisons were done with the Student Newman-Keuls procedure. On dichotomous variables χ^2 was employed.

Intake and Dropout

An examination of demographic characteristics at intake indicated that individuals who completed treatment did not differ systematically. In addition, similar proportions in each of these three groups were married ($\chi^2(2)$ = 4.14, $p < 0.15$) and employed ($\chi^2(2)$ = 3.16, $p < 0.20$)—about 45% were married and 70% were employed. Likewise none of the dependent variables showed differences at intake, indicating successful randomization. The number of clients who began the program in the professional, nonprofessional, and control groups was 48, 42, and 31, respectively. For purposes of filling the treatment groups the control group was not assigned any more Ss after N = 31. From this sample of 121 men, 51 failed to complete at least 10 therapy sessions and the outcome testing. Thus the outcome testing was completed on 26 professional, 25 nonprofessional, and 19 control clients. There was no significant difference in the dropout rates ($\chi^2(2)$ = 0.35, $p < 0.95$).

Treatment

One reason for using nonprofessional psychotherapeutic agents is the expectation that client accessibility to therapists will be increased. Table 34 contains the professional-nonprofessional comparisons relevant to this argument. The mean number of sessions and the time required to complete treatment are indicated. As suggested by the accessibility argument, the nonprofessional therapist had more sessions with his clients. Also, these sessions tended (p = 0.10) to occur more frequently. The nonprofessional appears to have been more available to clients than professional therapists were. However, it may be that professional therapists are more efficient, that is, they required fewer sessions and tended to use less total time (p = 0.06) to reach termination. Given the greater experience and training of professionals, greater efficiency in psychotherapy would be hoped for and seems to have some support. Finally, professional-nonprofessional therapist ratings of client improvement did not differ.

Outcome

Groups were compared at intake, outcome, 3-month follow-up, and 12-month follow-up. As in many programs that focus on problem drinking, primary outcome measures involved the effect of therapy on drinking behavior. Thus primary outcome measures included: a) number of days in past 90 without alcohol, b) mean ounces of 100% ethanol consumed per day when drinking, and c) frequency of "controlled" drinking, i.e., stopping after one or two drinks. Visual inspection suggested that all groups (including control) had improved during the time period of treatment. A treatment

Table 34. Means and standard deviations for treatment comparisons and therapist ratings

	Nonprofessional	Professional	t (49)
Treatment comparisons			
Number of clients	25	26	
Sessions	27.64	19.69	4.17[a]
(SD)	(5.06)	(8.15)	
Days between sessions	9.21	12.00	1.66[b]
(SD)	(3.22)	(7.79)	
Days between first and last session	243.20	201.08	
(SD)	(64.28)	(87.62)	
Therapist ratings[c]			
Number of clients[d]	23	23	
Resolution of "major complaint"[c]	2.09	2.00	1.21[e]
(SD)	(1.00)	(0.91)	

[a] $p < 0.01$.

[b] $p < 0.10$.

[c] Rated on 3-point scale: 1, "no improvement"; 2, "some improvement"; 3, "significant improvement."

[d] Difference in N is due to missing data.

[e] df = 46.

by time-repeated measures ANOVA confirmed this from intake to outcome with regard to these three drinking variables. We would have preferred that the control group not improve so much, thus yielding treatment (or therapist status) group differences and, more important, treatment by time interactions in this analysis. However, when the three variables were subjected to a multivariate ANOVA, there was clear indication that clients with therapy had improved more than the control group (F (6, 116) = 2.32, p < .05). Table 35 contains group means, univariate F ratios, and the results from orthogonal comparisons.

Univariate analyses on the drinking questions extended these analyses. To the yes/no question "Have you been drinking less (in the last 3 months)?" the nonprofessional group was significantly better than the control group in a posteriori analysis after an overall difference at the p = 0.004 level. All of the nonprofessional group members said "yes," whereas only half of the control indicated that they were drinking less. (The professional group was in between and not significantly different from either of the other two.)

On the question indicating the number of times that a subject had stopped after one or two drinks the overall analysis was significant (p = 0.03), but because of variances, a posteriori analyses were not. The pattern of means is obvious, however; the mean values of number of times stopped after one or two drinks were:

Professional—3.64
Nonprofessional—3.52
Control—2.44

On the item indicating the number of days drinking in the past 3 months the overall analysis approached significance ($p = 0.06$) and the a posteriori analyses indicated that the professional group was significantly better than the control. The means are indicators that treatment was obviously better than no treatment. The total numbers of days drinking in the past 90 days were as follows:

Professional—19.24
Nonprofessional—27.96
Control—43.05

(The professional and control groups differed by $p < 0.05$ in the Student Neuman-Keuls procedure.)

It was also indicated in the reasons for drinking that the treatment

Table 35.   Means and standard deviations for reported drinking behavior at intake and outcome

Time period	Nonprofessional ($N = 24$)[a]	Professional ($N = 24$)	Control ($N = 15$)	$F(2,60)$[b]
Intake				
Days without alcohol	39.87	50.00	45.53	< 1
(SD)	(30.01)	(29.04)	(27.77)	
Ethanol per day	5.89	5.02	7.63	
(SD)	(8.54)	(6.50)	(7.49)	< 1
Controlled drinking[c]	2.21	2.42	2.27	
(SD)	(1.10)	(1.39)	(1.22)	< 1
Outcome				
Days without alcohol	55.13[e]	72.83[d]	51.93[e]	
(SD)	(36.03)	(25.75)	(32.92)	2.70
Ethanol per day	1.71[d]	2.36[d]	5.93[e]	
(SD)	(3.50)	(6.87)	(9.47)	2.04
Controlled drinking	3.50[d]	3.71[d]	2.53[e]	
(SD)	(1.32)	(1.49)	(1.81)	2.99

[a] N differs from previous analyses because of missing data.

[b] If $F(2,60) = 2.39, p = 0.10$. If $F(2,60) = 3.15, p = 0.05$.

[c] Self-report of the frequency of the client stopping after one or two drinks. A 5-point scale was employed: 1, never; 2, very few times; 3, sometimes; 4, many times; 5, abstinent.

[d,e] Indicate results from orthogonal comparisons. Means with different superscripts differ significantly at 0.05.

Table 36.   Intake and outcome legal scores[a]

Time	Nonprofessional	Professional	Control	$F(2,67)$
Intake	10.96	11.19	12.05	0.62
(SD)	(2.84)	(3.69)	(3.49)	
Outcome	7.60	7.12	10.05	
(SD)	(1.96)	(3.41)	(4.33)	4.84[b]

[a] High scores indicate more legal involvement.

[b] $p < 0.05$.

groups, especially the nonprofessional group, found it less important to drink for social reasons.

At outcome, besides (or because of) reduced drinking, it was hoped that there would be positive changes in other areas of life, especially these men's involvement with the legal system. There were changes; Table 36 shows their overall legal scores.

The legal score was composed of a number of related items, i.e., times picked up by police ($p = 0.02$), times in jail ($p = 0.04$), number of court appearances ($p = 0.07$), and number of times guilty ($p = 0.01$). In each case the two treated groups were not different from each other but were significantly better than the control group in a posteriori comparisons.

Follow-up

Three months after the end of treatment our men were contacted and interviewed again. The treated groups were more likely to have had dry days ($p = 0.03$), and again had stopped more times after one or two drinks ($p = 0.033$). The treated groups were more likely to own a car ($p = 0.004$) and be living with someone ($p = 0.02$). The control group indicated that it was more important for them to drink to relax ($p = 0.01$) and to cheer themselves up ($p = 0.02$), whereas the treated groups indicated that these reasons were not important. The treated groups were not significantly different from each other on these variables.

At 12 months there were only three significant differences. The nonprofessional group had a few members who had sought help in an alcohol treatment center, whereas none in the professionally treated groups had done so ($p = 0.03$). In terms of drinking, the treated groups maintained some of their superiority. The average number of drinks when drinking ($p = 0.06$) were:

Professional—2.22
Nonprofessional—4.22
Control—9.01

(Professional and control groups differed by $p < 0.05$ in Student Neuman-

Keuls procedure.) The total numbers of days drinking in past 90 days were (p = 0.01):

Professional—18.88
Nonprofessional—26.59
Control—46.25

Both of the treated groups were significantly different from the control in the a posteriori analyses.

Arrest Records

The two treated groups were compared with the control during three time periods on the following categories of arrest:drunkenness, driving while intoxicated, total alcohol-related changes, disorderly conduct, and total charges. There were no significant differences between groups 1 year before and 1 year after treatment. However, during treatment drunkenness arrests (p = 0.06) and total alcoholic changes (p = 0.07) approached significance. In both cases the treated groups had one-half or less of the number of arrests than the control group. This is not a strong result because of the time period differences between groups—the treated groups had less time to collect their arrests—but it may indicate that treatment attention has an effect on reducing the amount of trouble these subjects encounter.

DISCUSSION

Overall these analyses clearly indicate a positive evaluation of treatment over no treatment. During treatment (and following, to a lesser degree) individuals who received rational psychotherapy systematically reported reduced drinking and legal difficulties more than a nontreated comparison group. However, despite reported improvements in the drinking and legal areas, other indications of economic and social functioning were not affected as much. Apparently the effects of treatment in this sample were mostly limited to those areas closest to the problem initially involving them in the program. Since rational psychotherapy is a problem-oriented approach and this was short-term treatment, often under coercion, this is not too surprising.

The more important aspect of the current study was the comparison of the professional and nonprofessional therapists, who both used the same approach to therapy. The nonprofessional therapist had more sessions with each client and had sessions more frequently than the professional therapist; he was more available to his clients. Moreover, on most measures of change at outcome the nonprofessional functioned as effectively as the professional. Conversely, the professionals were able to get as good results with less time involvement. During follow-up there was some indication that the nonprofessional group deteriorated slightly more than the professional group in their drinking behavior. Perhaps this was because of their greater dependence on their therapist, which was not as well resolved during treatment. These analyses suggest that continued reliance on nonprofessional therapists is advisable in treatment and should be "built in" in some form during follow-up.

Only one nonprofessional therapist was employed in this study. Despite his using a very structured set of therapy techniques, which mitigates against the results being due to his unique attributes, the design of the study does not allow one to partial out the effects of his personality. Thus, although in concert these results are very suggestive, they are not definitive, and additional studies are needed.

Nevertheless, self-help has long been the hope of the alcoholic. Other data from this project (see Chapter 7) indicate that this form of self-help was at least as effective as AA, and in some ways more so. It would seem that nonprofessionally administered rational therapy has support as a useful treatment for those who do not seem to benefit from other modalities, including AA.

chapter 9
SUMMARY AND
CONCLUSIONS

A review of the current treatment literature for the problems of alcoholism indicates an increasing sophistication in the expanding corpus of knowledge in this area. This study was undertaken in 1972 as an attempt to implement in design and sophistication a study to assess the effects of four different kinds of psychotherapy, with two of a self-help variety, and a control group in a comparative study. Random assignment of clients, multivariate outcome measures, and a 1-year follow-up procedure were important design characteristics of this study. Clients were recruited from the court system and, to a lesser extent, self-referrals were accepted.

Five hundred thirty-two subjects were screened, and of these 260 were accepted into the project. There were no differences between these two groups in alcohol consumption or signs of mental illness. However, the accepted clients were less organically impaired, admitted to more problems with drinking, and were brighter, younger, and more socially involved. As a group, those accepted were definitely alcoholic, of low-normal intelligence, and most had legal troubles.

Of the 260 that were accepted, 197 attended one session of therapy and only 116 completed treatment (at least 10 sessions) and some follow-up. Those that dropped out tended to prefer liquor over wine or beer, admitted to less aggregated problems, and had more severe problems with recent memory (denial and organicity). All demographic and behavioral measures indicated that randomization had been successful.

Main results at outcome included:

1. AA had the most dropouts.
2. AA and pro-RBT had the least number of sessions for subjects who did not drop out.
3. Insight and Pro-RBT groups did better in owning a car.
4. The insight therapy group had fewest legal problems overall. All treatments did better than the control in self-reported and objective measures of legal attention (arrests).
5. Insight therapy and Pro-RBT were best in the drinking index of total days dry.
6. On most drinking indices treatment of any type was superior to the control group.
7. On various behavioral indices treatment of any type was superior to the

control, although the variable showing significance would change over the various time periods.

Follow-up on the BRS measures indicated that most beneficial changes were occurring or continuing by the 3-month follow-up period. There was little consistency in the variables that were significant and only one significant result at the 12-month period. Despite changes in the significant dependent variables, treated groups always did better than the control subjects.

Repeated measures analyses were performed where appropriate to assess changes over time. In comparison to the other groups the lay-RBT group reported less importance attached to drinking in order to relax. The other significant results indicated that all groups (including the control group) changed over time in the following ways:

1. Less need to drink when nervous, to be cheered up
2. More able to stop drinking after one or two drinks
3. Work for alcohol (button presses) decreased at outcome but increased at 12-month follow-up
4. Driving while intoxicated charges decreased over follow-up

Repeated measures analyses on the MMPI indicated the following:

1. Hypochondriasis Scale decreased:
   For pro-RBT during treatment
   For lay-RBT during treatment and follow-up
   For insight therapy during follow-up
2. Hysteria Scale
   Increased for AA throughout treatment and follow-up
   Decreased for lay-RBT throughout treatment and follow-up
   Decreased for insight therapy during follow-up
3. Addiction Scale
   Decreased for pro-RBT during treatment
   Increased for lay-RBT during treatment
   Increased for AA during follow-up
4. Over time all groups decreased in psychopathy and anxiety, and increased in social desirability during treatment. All decreased their introversion during follow-up. General maladjustment of the type often found in alcoholics decreased during treatment and follow-up.

Further statistical analyses were performed on selected subgroups to investigate certain questions of interest. It was found that imported professional therapists were effective in cost, motivation, and results.

Using our project social worker in the role of a parole officer, it was found that legal coercive pressures were effective in increasing attendance and decreasing drinking and legal troubles at outcome, and in decreasing objective drunkenness arrests during follow-up. In many ways this group matched the performance of the volunteer subjects, indicating that external motivation when applied effectively is as effective as internal motivation.

Self-help methods proved useful, with the lay-RBT group having some advantages over traditional AA. Although not conclusive, the non-professional therapist was generally as successful as the professionals in administering the same kind of structured therapy.

The general decline of significant results during this follow-up period was partially determined by the "natural" improvement of the control group. However, these results also indicate a need for long-term, supportive treatment of alcoholics, perhaps most economically found in various self-help methods.

At times it has been difficult to characterize the complexity of our results, because highly consistent and significant results across individual measures and time periods were not evident. We chose a difficult population to study ("revolving door alcoholics") and on an absolute scale the outcomes were not outstanding, although they were well within the range of improvement reported in other studies. We believe that our data do warrant some overall conclusions despite the complexity of applying laboratory methodology to open systems over a long period of time. Treatment (of at least 10 sessions duration) will tend to help a man with alcohol problems with his drinking primarily, and also with his legal, behavioral, and general maladjustment problems. Comparatively, treatments did differentiate from each other in terms of dropouts (AA was clearly the worst), legal problems (insight therapy seemed best), and the total days dry (professional groups were superior). However, the general thrust was that treatment of any kind was superior to no treatment at all, even though the control subjects tended to get better over time on most variables as well.

Any empirical study, no matter what its scope or defects, must be judged by its utility in confirmation or extension of existing knowledge, both data and theory oriented. It is hoped that this study makes a contribution in this regard. There seems to be an emerging consensus in the fields both of psychotherapy research and psychotherapeutic alcoholism treatment that most persons improve with treatment and would not improve without it. In the field of alcoholism this may mean continued drinking, but at lower levels, and in a much less problematic way. Although all forms of treatment have not been compared, it seems likely that different types of psychotherapy do not have large, differentiated effects, at least not large enough to argue about or to obviate "bottom line" concerns of cost effectiveness. In this regard the most cost-effective methods may become certain combinations of self-help, perhaps with professional consultation and detoxification available. Attitudes toward alcohol and community organization will have to be improved to provide a context for effective treatment. Since getting a minimum of whatever kind of treatment seems essential theoretically and has been demonstrated empirically, the use of efficient coercive pressures seems warranted and should be further explored legally and therapeutically.

APPENDICES

appendix A
AUTHORIZATION
FORM—VOLUNTARY CLIENTS

SHARP
Self-Help Alcoholism Research Project
University of Kentucky
Department of Psychiatry

Consent for Treatment and/or Testing

This project provides treatment for persons with alcohol-related problems. All of the treatments are currently popular and widely used. You will *not* be charged for any treatment.

Since a research project cannot treat all applicants, you may *not* be accepted for treatment. However, whether accepted or not, you will be expected to make pertinent information available to the research staff, first to determine your eligibility, and then after a year has elapsed.

This later testing period will include some form of follow-up every 3 months during a 1-year period. For this, with your consent, you will be paid a sum which in total will not exceed $85.00.

OR

I have read and understand the above statements, and I do hereby give my consent to the University of Kentucky Department of Psychiatry and the staff of the Self-Help Alcoholism Research Project to use those procedures and practices appropriate for treatment and testing. I also anticipate that treatment may last up to 1 year and I plan to stay within the program for that length of time.

_____

Signature of Client

_____

Date

_____

Witness

_____

Witness

appendix B
COURT REFERRAL FORM

Date: _____

TO: Self-Help Alcoholism Research Project
     431 S. Broadway, Suite 312
     Lexington, Kentucky 40508

RE: WRC Case No. _____

In lieu of a jail sentence for the herein described offense _____
_____, the person named below has been referred to
SHARP, to satisfy the judgment of this Court.

> NAME: _____
>
> ADDRESS: _____
>
> CITY & STATE: _____
>
> TELEPHONE NO.: _____
>
> OPR. LIC. NO.: _____
>
> SOC. SEC. NO.: _____
>
> DATE OF BIRTH: _____

Pursuant your blanket instructions for referrals (any hour Monday through Friday, 9 am to 5 pm, and on Tuesday and Thursday, 6–8 pm) we have set his initial appointment for:

DAY: _____ DATE: _____ TIME: _____

In the event he should fail to appear for his initial appointment or should become delinquent in his attendance or fail to cooperate with Project personnel in any manner disruptive or adverse to his treatment or that of others, or should he do any other thing which is contrary to the purpose and intent of his participation in this program, such conduct should be reported in writing to this Court detailing the conduct complained of and containing recommendations or suggestions for action to be taken by the Court.

Acceptance of this Referral should be made in writing to the Court, as should dismissals at the end of the treatment period. Interim reports should be made by Self-Help at their discretion and/or on request by the Court.

The person referred to this Project may petition this Court for a hearing for relief or changes in the attendance requirement by reporting any instances of misconduct by, or disagreements with, Project personnel, or by stating other reasons why such relief should be granted.

The Court maintains, at all times, the final decision as to whether the Referral has satisfactorily completed the program.

Sincerely,

Judge

appendix C
LEGAL CONTRACT FORM

SHARP
Self-Help Alcoholism Research Project
University of Kentucky
Department of Psychiatry

CONTRACT

I, _____, convicted of the offense of
_____ in the City Court, do hereby
agree to enter the SHARP Project, a treatment program for persons with
alcohol-related problems, in lieu of a jail sentence, imposed on me by the
Court.

I fully understand the said program, and will co-operate with the
SHARP staff during testing and treatment. I understand also that treatment may run over a period of 30 to 45 weeks, and that I will comply with
the follow-up work of the program after treatment is completed.

It is further understood that, should I withdraw my cooperation from
the program, the presiding judge or prosecuting attorney will be notified,
and I will have to serve the jail sentence initially imposed or whatever
sentence the judge so decrees.

_____
Referral

_____
SHARP Staff Member

On _____, there appeared before me _____
    day   month   year
_____, of _____,
known to me to be the person therein, under oath affixed his signature to
the Contract with a SHARP representative.

I, _____, a notary public in and for
the state at large do hereby affix my seal to said document, on this
_____.
    day   month   year

_____
Notary

(SEAL)

appendix D
MENTAL STATUS INTERVIEW

Accept _____   Name _____
Reject _____   Date _____

1. Age _____ Education _____ Marital Status _____
2. Occupation _____ Presently Employed _____ Where _____
3. Do you reside in Lexington or surrounding county? _____
   How long have you lived at your present address? _____
   Address _____ Phone Number _____
4. With whom do you reside at the present time? _____
   How long have you been together? _____
5. Do you have your own means of transportation? _____
   Would you have a way to get to the U.K. Medical Center at least once a week?
6. What is the offense with which you have been charged? _____
   A. After taking one or two drinks, can you usually stop drinking without diffi-
      culty? _____
   B. When not drinking, have you ever heard voices when there was no one
      around? _____
      When not drinking, have you ever seen things that later turned out not to
      be there? _____
      When not drinking, have you ever smelled something that had no apparent
      source? _____
   C. Do you ever forget what you just heard or saw? _____
      Do you ever forget what you are trying to say? _____
      Do you have trouble remembering things from a few months back? _____
   D. Do you often experience extreme happiness or extreme sadness? _____
      What is it like? _____

SCREENING INTERVIEW

   E. Do you think any person or group of persons is against you or is out to get
      you? _____
   F. What does the word *religion* mean to you? _____
   G. What does the word *marriage* mean to you? _____
   H. Why do you think things happen in the world the way they do?
      _____
   I. Who is the U.S. President? _____ Who was before him?
      _____
   J. Who is the Governor of Ky.? _____ The mayor of Lexington?
      _____
   K. Where were you born? _____
   L. The date of your birth? _____

AFFECT: Appropriate _____ Inappropriate _____
SPEECH: Intelligible _____ Unintelligible _____
DELUSIONS: Present _____ Absent _____
HALLUCINATIONS: Present _____ Absent _____
MEMORY PROBLEMS: *Recent* None _____ Mild _____ Severe _____
                  Remote None _____ Mild _____ Severe _____

Person Testing

appendix E
DRINKING QUESTIONNAIRE AND SCORING KEY

```
NAME _____
ID #_____
AGE  _____  Years
WEIGHT _____  lb
```

DRINKING QUESTIONNAIRE (DQ)—KEY

Major Physiological Index

1. When you stop drinking have you ever had . . .
   a. tremors (the shakes)   _____ Yes = 2 pts
                                                      Yes,   No

   b. seizures (convulsion or fit)   _____ Yes = 2 pts
                                                      Yes,   No

   c. hallucinations (seeing or hearing things not there)
                                                     _____ Yes = 2 pts
                                                      Yes,   No

   d. DTs (to include tremors, disorientation, hallucinations, etc.)
                                                     _____ Yes = 2 pts
                                                      Yes,   No

2. When you drink . . .
   a. How much do you usually drink *per day*?

	Beer (4%)			Wine (20%)			Hard liquor (43%)			
	Tap glass (7 oz)	Bottle or can (12 oz)	Quart (32 oz)	Glass (4 oz)	Fifth (25.6 oz)	Quart (32 oz)	Shot (1 oz)	Pint (16 oz)	Fifth (25.6 oz)	Quart (32 oz)
Number of →										
Multiply by →	0.28	0.48	1.28	0.8	5.12	6.4	0.43	6.93	11.01	13.76
Product →										

Sum of products _____ oz
(oz of 100% ethyl alcohol)

Consumption requirement for alcohol tolerance

Weight of individual (lb)	Minimum consumption of 100% ethyl alcohol (oz)
220	13.76
200	12.38
180	11.01
160	9.63
140	8.26
120	6.88

b.   How many days in a row do you drink the above amount

_____ days

(If the individual's consumption of 100% ethyl alcohol (his sum of products) on part "a" of question 2 is equal to or greater than the minimum consumption rate indicated for his body weight *and* if the subject's answer to part "b" of question 2 is equal to or greater than 2, then question 2 is awarded 2 points.)

Consumption and time requirements met—2 points

3.   Have you ever had blackouts when you have been drinking?

_____ Yes = 1 pt

Yes,   No

Major Behavioral, Psychological, and Attitudinal Index

4.   Has your medical doctor strongly advised you not to drink because drinking will damage your health?

_____ Yes = 2 pts

Yes,   No

5.   Have you ever . . .
a.   lost a job because of your drinking? _____

Yes,   No

b.   had problems in your marriage because of your drinking?_____

Yes,   No

c.   been arrested for any alcohol-related offenses? _____

Yes,   No

(If subject answers Yes to any or all of question 5, 2 pts. total are awarded.)

Affirmative answer/s = 2 pts

6.   Do you feel you can stop drinking after taking one or two drinks?

_____ No = 1 pt

Yes,   No

Minor Behavioral, Psychological, and Attitudinal Index

7.   Have you ever tried to hide the fact that you were drinking from anyone?

_____ Yes = 1 pt

Yes,   No

8.   Do you ever drink in the morning?   _____ Yes = 1 pt

Yes,   No

9.   Have you lost interest in any activities that you used to be fairly interested in?

_____ Yes = 1 pt

Yes,   No

10. Have you ever become very angry or threatened suicide while drinking?

_____ Yes = 1 pt

Yes,   No

11. Does your wife (mother, girl friend, etc.) often complain about your drinking?

_____ Yes = 1 pt

Yes,   No

12. Do you think you drink to relieve anger, insomnia, fatigue, depression and/or social discomfort?

_____ Yes = 1 pt

Yes,   No

Major Physiological Index (MPI)[1] _____ of 11 pts possible.

(Q1 + Q2 + Q3)

Major Behavioral, Psychological, and Attitudinal Index (MBPAI)[1]

_____ of 5 pts. possible.

(Q4 + Q5 + Q6)

Minor Behavioral, Psychological, and Attitudinal Index (BPAI)[1]

_____ of 6 pts. possible.

(Q7 + Q8 + Q9 + Q10 + Q11 + Q12)

TOTAL = (MPI + MBPAI) + BPAI = _____ pts. of 22 pts. possible.

If MPI and MBPAI and BPAI $\geq$ 3, then subject *has met* criterion (passed) for inclusion in Alcoholic sample.

If MPI or MBPAI or BPAI $<$ 3, then subject *has not met* criterion (failed) for inclusion in Alcoholic sample.

The subject has _____ .

Passed = 1

Failed = 2

---

[1] Items based on National Council on Alcoholism, Criteria for the diagnosis of alcoholism, *Annals of Internal Medicine 77:*249–258, 1977.

appendix F
ALCOHOLISM CRITERIA

Alcoholism criteria from the National Council on Alcoholism (1972) used in the construction of the Drinking Questionnaire

Diagnostic level	National Council on Alcoholism criteria	Drinking Questionnaire item
	Physiological and Clinical—Track I (major criteria)	

1[a]   A. Physiological Dependency
        1. Physiological dependence as manifested by a *withdrawal syndrome* when intake of alcohol is interrupted . . .
           a. Gross tremor (differentiated from other causes of tremor)
           b. Hallucinosis (differentiated from szhizophrenia hallucinations or other psychoses)
           c. Withdrawal seizures (differentiated from epilepsy and other seizure disorders)
           d. Delirium tremors (usually start between first and third days after withdrawal and minimally include tremors, disorientation, and hallucinations)

1. When you stop drinking have you ever had:
    a. tremors (the shakes)
    b. hallucinations (seeing or hearing things not there)
    c. seizures (convulsion or fit)
    d. DT's (including tremors, disorientation, hallucinations, etc.)

1   2. Evidence of *tolerance* to the effects of alcohol . . .
           b. the consumption of ⅕ gallon of whiskey or an equivalent amount of wine or beer daily, for more than 1 day, by a 180-lb individual.

2. When you drink . . .
    a. How much do you usually drink *per day*? (record amount of each beverage and convert to ounces of 100% ethyl alcohol)
          _____ oz
    (oz of 100% ethyl alcohol)
    Is consumption greater than requirement?

Whiskey equivalents of consumption of wine or beer

Weight of individual	Whiskey	Fortified Wine	Table Wine	Beer Quart	Beer 12 oz
kg (lb)		qt			
100 (220)	1.0	2.0	3.6	11.0	29
91 (200)	0.9	1.9	3.2	9.7	26
82 (180)	0.8	1.7	2.9	8.6	23
73 (160)	0.7	1.5	2.5	7.5	20
64 (140)	0.6	1.3	2.2	6.5	17
54 (120)	0.5	1.0	1.8	5.4	14

Equivalents are based on: 0.8 quart = ⅕ gallon; 32 oz = 1 quart; whiskey contains 43% ethyl alcohol; fortified wine contains 20% ethyl alcohol; table wine contains 12% ethyl alcohol; beer contains 4% ethyl alcohol.

Consumption requirement for alcohol tolerance

Weight of individual (lb)	Min. consumption of 100% ethyl alcohol (oz)
220	13.76
200	12.38
180	11.01
160	9.63
140	8.26
120	6.88

2[b]   3. Alcoholic "blackout" periods (differential diagnosis from purely psychological fugue states and psychomotor seizures)

    b. How many days in a row do you drink the above amount?
        _____ days
3. Have you ever had blackouts when you have been drinking?

Behavioral, Psychological, and Attitudinal—Track II (major criteria)

1   The following behavior patterns show psychological dependence on alcohol in alcoholism.

1. Drinking despite strong medical contraindication known to patient

1   2. Drinking despite strong, identified social contradiction (job loss for intoxication, marriage disruption because of drinking, arrest for intoxication, driving while intoxicated)

2   3. Patients' subjective complaint of loss of control of alcohol consumption

4. Has your medical doctor strongly advised you not to drink because drinking will damage your health?

5. Have you ever . . .
   a. lost a job because of your drinking?
   b. had problems in your marriage because of your drinking?
   c. been arrested for any alcohol-related offenses?

6. Do you feel you can stop drinking after one or two drinks?

Behavioral, Psychological, and Attitudinal—Track II (minor criteria)

2   A. Behavioral
   1. Direct effects
      b. Early—Surreptitious drinking

2   c. Early—Morning drinking (assess nature of peer group behavior)

2   2. Indirect effects
   d. Early—Loss of interest in activities not directly associated with drinking

2   f. Late—Outbursts of rage and suicidal gestures while drinking

B. Psychological and Attitudinal
   1. Direct effects

2   a. Middle—Drinking to relieve anger, insomnia, fatigue, depression, social discomfort
   2. Indirect effects

2   b. Early—Spouse makes complaints about drinking behavior, reported by patient or spouse

7. Have you ever tried to hide the fact that you were drinking from anyone?

8. Do you ever drink in the morning?

9. Have you lost interest in any activities that you used to be fairly interested in?

10. Have you ever become very angry or threatened suicide while drinking?

12. Do you drink to relieve anger, insomnia, fatigue, depression, and/or social discomfort?

11. Does your wife (mother, girl friend, etc.) often complain about your drinking?

Items based on National Council on Alcoholism, Criteria for the diagnosis of alcoholism, *Annals of Internal Medicine* 77:249–258, 1972.

[a] Diagnostic Level 1—Classical, definite, obligatory. A person who fits this must be diagnosed as being alcoholic.

[b] Diagnostic Level 2—Probable, frequent, indicative. A person who satisfies this criterion is under strong suspicion of alcoholism; other corroborative evidence should be obtained.

appendix G
DIRECTION AND RATIONALE FOR SCORING OF THE MODIFIED GRAY ORAL READING TEST

Table G-1.   Paragraph Score

Seconds	Errors							
	0	1	2	3	4	5	6	7 or more
40 or more	4	4	3	2	1	0	0	0
30–39	4	4	3	2	1	1	1	0
25–29	4	4	3	2	2	1	1	0
20–24	4	4	3	3	2	1	1	0
19 or less	4	4	4	3	2	1	1	0

Since the entire Gray Oral Reading Paragraph Test (1955) was not given at the screening session, certain assumptions must be made based on the two paragraphs (#6 and #7) that were given to see if the S had or had not attained a sixth grade reading level.

PROCEDURE

1. Using Table G-1, Paragraph Score, from the Gray's *Direction for Scoring Test Papers*, convert the time and errors for paragraphs #6 and #7 to Raw Scores.
2. Assume that as the hardness of the 12 paragraphs increases (paragraph #1 = least hard, paragraph #12 = most hard) that the length of time and/or number of errors will increase. Thus the Raw Score will go from higher to lower.

Table G-2.   The B-Scores in terms of Raw Scores

Raw Score	B-Score	Raw Score	B-Score
1	1.4	18	4.2
2	1.6	19	4.4
3	1.8	20	4.5
4	1.9	21	4.7
5	2.1	22	4.9
6	2.3	23	5.1
7	2.4	24	5.2
8	2.6	25	5.4
9	2.8	26	5.7
10	2.9	27	5.9
11	3.1	28	6.1
12	3.2	29	6.4
13	3.4	30	6.7
14	3.6	31	7.0
15	3.7	32	7.3
16	3.9	33	7.7
17	4.0	34	8.0

3. Assume that the normal pattern of Raw Scores (from Table G-2) for a 6.1 B-Score is 444433221100 for a total Raw Score of 28.

4. Given this normal pattern, paragraph #6 has a Raw Score of 3 and paragraph #7 has a Raw Score of 2. Because of idiosyncratic behaviors of individuals within a given population there will be individuals that might have erratic patterns and still receive 28 Raw Score points and still have a minimum of a 6.1 B-Score. Thus instead of looking at the pattern of Raw Scores on paragraphs #6 and #7 (Raw Scores 3 and 2, respectively) the sum of the two scores will become the criterion for the minimum of a B-Score of 6.1.

5. Thus, if paragraph #6 Raw Score + paragraph #7 Raw Score is greater than or equal to 5, then the subject has at least a B-Score of 6.1 (at a sixth grade reading level). If his Raw Score is less than 5, then his B-Score is below 6 (reads below a sixth grade level).

6. The criterion for passing the Gray's Oral Reading Test is a sixth grade reading level. Thus S fails Reading Test if the combined Raw Scores of paragraphs #6 and #7 is below 5. S passes Reading Test if the combined Raw Score of paragraphs #6 and #7 is 5 or above.

appendix H
DEMOGRAPHIC
QUESTIONNAIRE

1. What is the highest level of school you have completed? (Circle one)

   1 Graduate professional   5 Partial high school
   2 College graduate   6 Junior high school
   3 Partial college   7 5–7 years of school
   4 High school graduate   8 Less than 5 years of school

Employment

2. What is your current occupation? (Give response and circle one below)

   1 Executive and/or proprietor of large concern; member of major profession
   2 Manager and/or proprietor of medium-size business—member of a minor profession
   3 Administrative personnel in large business; owner of small independent business; semi-professional
   4 Clerical or sales worker; technician
   5 Skilled manual worker
   6 Semi-skilled worker
   7 Unskilled worker
   8 None

3. What is your yearly gross income?

   1 Above $25,000   3 $11–15,000   5 $5100–7500   7 $0–3000
   2 $16–25,000   4 $7600–10,000 6 $3100–5000

4. Is your employment: part-time (   )   full time (   )
5. What is the length of time on your most recent job? _____
6. In your whole life what job did you hold for the longest time?_____
   How long? _____
7. List your job changes in the last 12 months starting with the most recent.

   _____

   _____

8. List your jobs in the past 6 years starting with the more recent (1 year ago).

   _____

   _____

9. Marital Information
   A. If married, presently or formerly, check one of the statements below
       1. Married, only one marriage (or remarried only one time as a consequence of death of spouse), living as a unit.
           ____a. Adequate heterosexual relations achieved.
           ____b. Low sexual drive, difficult sexual relations, or extramarital affairs, either partner.

2. Married, more than one time, maintained a home in one marriage for at least 5 years.

    _____a. Adequate sexual relations during at least one marriage.

    _____b. Chronically inadequate sexual life.

    _____c. Married and apparently permanently separated or divorced without remarriage, but maintained a home in one marriage for at least 5 years.

    _____d. Same as (c), but maintained a home in one marriage for *less than 5 years.*

B. If single, 30 years or over, check one of the statements below.

1. Have been engaged one or more times or have had a long-term relationship (at least 2 years) involving heterosexual relations or apparent evidence for a "love affair" with one person, but unable to achieve marriage.

2. Brief or short-term heterosexual or social dating experiences with one or more partners, but no long-lasting sexual experiences with a single partner.

3. Sexual and/or social relationships primarily with the same sex, but may have had occasional heterosexual contacts or dating experiences.

4. Minimal sexual or social interest in either men or women.

Go to question 10.

C. If single, under 30 years, i.e., 20–29, check one of the statements below.

1. Have had at least one long-term "love affair" (minimum of 6 months to 1 year) or engagement, even though religious or other prohibitions may have prevented actual sexual union.

    _____a. Have been actually engaged.

    _____b. Otherwise.

2. Brief or short-term heterosexual or social dating experiences, "love affairs," with one or more partners, but no long-lasting sexual experiences with a single partner.

3. Casual sexual or social relationships with persons of either sex, but may have had occasional heterosexual contacts or dating experiences.

4. Sexual and/or social relationships primarily with the same sex, but may have had occasional heterosexual contacts or dating experiences.

5. Minimal sexual or social interest in either men or women.

Go to question 10.

10. Do you live (check one) alone (   ) or with someone (   ) currently?

Man (   )   Woman (   )

What is your marital status? (Circle one)
1. Married
2. Common law
3. Separated
4. Divorced
5. Widowed—alone
6. Single—alone
11. Have you any history of psychiatric care? (Check as many as appropriate)
_____1 Counseling (Specify type _____)
_____2 Outpatient therapy
_____3 Hospitalization (Number of times _____)
12. What drugs (besides alcohol) have you used in the past 2 weeks?

Drug	Dosage	Frequency
_____	_____	_____
_____	_____	_____
_____	_____	_____

13. Do you have any blood relatives diagnosed or treated for mental illness?

Specify

1 Grandparents _____
2 Sibs _____
3 Father _____
4 Mother _____
5 Both parents_____
6 Parents and sibs _____
7 None _____

14. Do you have any blood relatives with a history of alcoholism?
1 Grandparents _____
2 Sibs _____
3 Father _____
4 Mother _____
5 Both parents_____
6 Parents and sibs _____
7 None _____

Legal

15. How many times have you been in trouble with the law?
Arrests _____
Misdemeanors _____
Felonies _____

16. How many traffic violations have you had in two years?

Check penalties

0	None	____Jail
1	One	____License revocation
2	Two	____License suspension
3	Five or less	____Fine
4	Five or more	____Warning

17. How many accidents in the last 5 years? (Circle one)

0   1   2   3   4   5

Drinking

18. About how old were you when you first started drinking (not counting small tastes of alcoholic beverages)? _____ Years

19. Between the ages of 14 and 21 did you drink heavily? _____

20. How old were you when you first got drunk? _____ Years

21. When you drink, do you drink everyday?

____1 No (Go to question 23)
____3 Yes, occasionally
____5 Yes, usually

22. Do you drink every day at a specific time?

____1 Never
____3 Yes, occasionally
____5 Yes, usually

23. When you drink, do you drink on weekends only?

____1 No
____3 Yes, occasionally
____5 Yes, usually

24. What would you say best describes your overall drinking habits?

____1 periodic, intermittent drinker (one who drinks heavily on a binge or drinking bout every so often, with periods of little or no drinking between binges) (Go to question 25, skip 26)
____3 steady, regular drinker (one who continually drinks more or less the same amount on a day-to-day basis) (Go to question 26)
____9 cannot say (or both) (Go to questions 25 and 26)

25. Periodic drinkers and cannot say group.

A. About how long does your average drinking bout last? _____
B. What is the longest bout you have ever had? _____
C. On the average, how much time goes by between drinking bouts?
D. What main factor determines when one of these drinking bouts ends?

____1 Become too sick to go on (or pass out)
____2 Someone else forces me to stop

_____3   Run out of money

_____4   I no longer feel a need to drink

_____5   I decide to stop

_____6   Other (explain)_____

_____9   Don't know

(Go to question 27)

26. Steady drinkers and cannot say group.

Are there any particular days of the week during which you drink more than on other days?   _____Yes   _____No

_____1   Monday, Tuesday

_____2   Wednesday, Thursday

_____5   Friday, Saturday, Sunday

_____7   No particular days

27. Since drinking first became a real problem, what is the longest period of time during which you did not take a drink?

_____1   Length of time (Write in)   _____

_____2   No dry periods (Go to question 29)

28. What was the main factor associated with your stopping drinking and becoming dry at that time?

_____1   Became too sick to go on (or passed out)

_____2   Someone else forced me to stop

_____3   Ran out of money

_____4   I no longer felt a need to drink

_____5   I decided to stop

_____6   Other (Explain)   _____

_____9   Don't know

29. Have you ever drunk alcoholic substitutes (such as canned heat, hair tonic, shaving lotion, cough syrup)?

_____1   No (Go to question 30)

_____3   Yes, once a year or less

_____5   Yes, more than once a year

30. How much food do you eat while you are drinking?

_____1 None	_____4 Heavy meal
_____2 Snacks	_____5 Other (Explain) _____
_____3 Regular meal	_____9 Don't know

31. Instead of alcohol, have you ever used drugs or medicines, such as sleeping pills, pep pills, tranquilizers, reefers, narcotics, hallucinogens?

_____1   No

_____3   Yes (Explain)   _____

32. Do you ever have a "blackout" (a loss of memory without loss of consciousness) in connection with your drinking? If so, how often?

_____1 No (Go to question 34)	_____7 Every time I drink
_____3 Yes, occasionally	_____9 Don't know
_____5 Yes, frequently	

33. About how long did your last blackout last?

   ____1   1–60 minutes   ____4   1–4 weeks

   ____2   1–24 hours   ____5   More than a month

   ____3   1–6 days   ____9   Don't know

34. After a drinking bout, have you ever had the shakes?

   ____1   No

   ____3   Yes

   ____9   Don't know

35. After a drinking bout have you ever had convulsions?

   ____1   No   ____7   Yes, every time I drink

   ____3   Yes, occasionally   ____9   Don't know

   ____5   Yes, frequently

36. After a drinking bout, have you ever had DTs (seen, felt, or heard things not really there)?

   ____1   No   ____7   Yes, every time I drink

   ____3   Yes, occasionally   ____9   Don't know

   ____5   Yes, frequently

37. How long on the average do you sleep each day when you are drinking?

   ____1   Less than 2 hours   ____5   From 8 to 10 hours

   ____2   From 3 to 4 hours   ____6   More than 10 hours

   ____3   From 5 to 6 hours   ____9   Don't know

   ____4   From 7 to 8 hours

38. How long do you sleep when you are *not* drinking?

   ____1   Less than 2 hours   ____5   From 5 to 10 hours

   ____2   From 3 to 4 hours   ____6   More than 10 hours

   ____3   From 5 to 6 hours   ____9   Don't know

   ____4   From 7 to 8 hours

39. In your opinion, is your drinking problem getting progressively worse?

   ____1   No

   ____3   Yes

   ____9   Don't know

40. Do you feel you need help for your problem with alcohol?

   ____1   No, I don't need help

   ____3   Yes, I do need help

   ____5   I don't have a problem

appendix I
PROBLEM CHECKLIST

Check any of the following that apply to you.

( ) headaches

( ) dizziness

( ) fainting spells

( ) palpitations

( ) stomach trouble

( ) no appetite

( ) bowel disturbance

( ) fatigue

( ) trouble sleeping

( ) nightmares

( ) take sedatives

( ) alcoholism

( ) feel tense

( ) feel panicky

( ) tremors

( ) depressed

( ) suicidal ideas

( ) always worried about something

( ) unable to relax

( ) unable to have a good time

( ) don't like weekends and vacations

( ) overambitious

( ) sexual problems

( ) shy with people

( ) can't make friends

( ) can't make decisions

( ) can't keep a job

( ) inferiority feelings

( ) home conditions bad

( ) financial problems

( ) stubbornness

( ) clumsiness

( ) forgetfulness

( ) mood changes

( ) lonliness

( ) temper tantrums

( ) suspiciousness

( ) guilt feelings

( ) loss of interest

( ) confusion

( ) irritability

( ) parental problems

( ) legal problems

( ) problems with relatives

( ) problems with in-laws

appendix J
CRAVING AND WITHDRAWAL QUESTIONNAIRE

CRAVING QUESTIONS

1. After taking one or more drinks do you find it hard to stop drinking?
    1   No
    2   Yes, sometimes
    3   Yes, frequently
2. Have you ever worried because you fear you may not have a drink when you need it?
    1   No
    2   Yes, sometimes
    3   Yes, frequently
3. When you are drinking, do you usually have a bottle by your bedside?
    1   No
    2   Yes, sometimes
    3   Yes, frequently
4. When you are sober, do you constantly think about drinking and/or alcohol?
    1   No
    2   Yes, sometimes
    3   Yes, frequently
5. When you are sober, do you sometimes find yourself taking a drink or about to take a drink without realizing it?
    1   No
    2   Yes, sometimes
    3   Yes, frequently
6. When you are sober, do you ever have a "dry drunk," i.e., act or feel like you were drunk when you had nothing to drink?
    1   No
    2   Yes, sometimes
    3   Yes, frequently
7. When you are sober, do you "plan" drunks?
    1   No
    2   Yes, sometimes
    3   Yes, frequently
8. When you are sober, does it make you want to drink when you are around people who are drinking?
    1   No
    2   Yes, sometimes
    3   Yes, frequently
9. When you are sober, do you avoid places where alcohol is likely to be found?
    1   No
    2   Yes, sometimes
    3   Yes, frequently

10. When you are dry, to what extent do you think about alcohol?
    1   Not at all
    2   A little
    3   A fair amount
    4   Very much

11. When you are dry and you smell alcohol or see someone drinking, to what extent can you taste it?
    1   Not at all
    2   A little
    3   A fair amount
    4   Very much

12. When you are dry and you walk by a tavern, to what extent do you experience a "need" for a drink?
    1   Not at all
    2   A little
    3   A fair amount
    4   Very much

13. When you are dry and around alcohol, to what extent do you feel shaky, nervous, or jumpy?
    1   Not at all
    2   A little
    3   A fair amount
    4   Very much

14. When you are dry, to what extent do you have the feeling that you really don't feel "normal" unless you have some alcohol?
    1   Not at all
    2   A little
    3   A fair amount
    4   Very much

15. When you are drinking steadily, how difficult is it for you to voluntarily stop drinking?
    1   Not at all
    2   A little
    3   A fair amount
    4   Very much

16. When you are drinking steadily, to what extent does it feel like your body craves or needs alcohol?
    1   Not at all
    2   A little
    3   A fair amount
    4   Very much

17. When you are drinking steadily and you awaken after a sleep, how often is getting a drink the first thing you think about?
    1   Not at all

    2 A little
    3 A fair amount
    4 Very much

18. When you are drinking steadily and you find yourself in a situation where you can't get alcohol, how desperate for a drink do you feel?
    1 Not at all
    2 A little
    3 A fair amount
    4 Very much

19. After drinking for some time, when you stop, or are forced to stop, to what extent do you feel shaky and nervous?
    1 Not at all
    2 A little
    3 A fair amount
    4 Very much

WITHDRAWAL QUESTIONS

1. Have you had a convulsion (fit) when sobering up?
    1 No
    2 Yes, sometimes
    3 Yes, frequently

2. Have you ever had "shakes," i.e., hands tremble, shake inside, when sobering up?
    1 No
    2 Yes, sometimes
    3 Yes, frequently

3. When coming off a drunk, have you "seen" things that were not there?
    1 No
    2 Yes, sometimes
    3 Yes, frequently

4. When coming off a drunk, have you heard "things" that were not there?
    1 No
    2 Yes, sometimes
    3 Yes, frequently

5. When coming off a drunk do you have vague feelings or anxieties?
    1 No
    2 Yes, sometimes
    3 Yes, frequently

6. When sobering up, have you been overly hot and/or sweaty (feverish)?
    1 No
    2 Yes, sometimes
    3 Yes, frequently

7. When sobering up, have you felt "things" crawling on you that were not there?
    1 No
    2 Yes, sometimes
    3 Yes, frequently

8. When sobering up, have you had weird or frightening sensations?
    1 No
    2 Yes, sometimes
    3 Yes, frequently

9. When sobering up have you felt your heart beating very rapidly?
    1 No
    2 Yes, sometimes
    3 Yes, frequently

10. After a drinking bout have you ever had DTs?
    1 No
    2 Yes, sometimes
    3 Yes, frequently

11. After a drinking bout have you been afraid you might have DTs?
    1 No
    2 Yes, sometimes
    3 Yes, frequently

12. Have you had blackouts (loss of memory without passing out)?
    1 No
    2 Yes, sometimes
    3 Yes, frequently

13. If you have had blackouts, what is the longest time they've lasted?
    0 Never had one
    1 Less than an hour
    2 For several hours
    3 For a day or more

appendix K
BEHAVIOR RATING SCALE AND SCORING KEYS—SOCIAL, EMPLOYMENT, ECONOMIC, AND LEGAL

1. a. At the present time do you live alone or with someone?

   ____Alone   ____With someone

   b. Where do you live?

   ____My own house, trailer, or other owned quarters.

   ____Rented (or provided) house, apartment, or trailer (with cooking facilities).

   ____Rented (or provided) room, hotel, boarding house (without cooking facilities).

   ____Other (Explain) _____

2. In the past 3 months (or since we last saw you) how many times have you changed your home address, if at all?

   ____0–1 Move   ____2 Moves   ____3 or more moves

3. How many meals per day do you usually eat? ____ Where do you eat?

Meal	Home where I live	Work	Other
Breakfast			
Lunch (mid-day)			
Supper			
Other			

   ____all at work or other

   ____all at home

   ____some at home, some at work or other

4. In the past 3 weeks have you usually eaten _____ by yourself or with someone? If with someone, do you usually know the person well?

Meal	Alone	With someone	Know well Yes	No
Breakfast				
Lunch (mid-day)				
Supper				
Other				

   ____2 or more with someone

   ____1 with someone

   ____0 with someone

5. In how many different places have you spent the night during the past month?

   ____0–1 place   ____4 places

   ____2 places   ____5 places

   ____3 places   ____6 or more places

6. How many really close friends (including relatives) would you say you have at this time? _____

   ____None   ____1 or more

7. How many of those friends have you talked to in the past week?

   ____None   ____ 1 or more

8. How often in the past week have you gone out of your way to meet one of these friends? For example, by calling him, going to his house, going across the street to talk to him?
   ____None   ____1 or more

9. a. Do you belong to any organizations, clubs, groups or churches (excluding AA)?
      ____No (Go to question 10)   ____Yes
      If yes:
   b. Which ones? _____
   c. How many of these have you joined in the past 3 months (or since we last saw you)? _____
   d. Do you serve as an officer in any of these groups?
      ____No   ____Yes
   e. On the average, how many times each month do you go to meeting of these groups?

10. Are you presently affiliated with Alcoholics Anonymous?
    ____No   ____Yes

11. In the last 3 months (or since we last saw you), on the average, how many scheduled AA meetings per month have you attended (or total number of meetings in specified time period)? _____

12. a. In the last 3 months (or since we last saw you) were there any times you stopped by an AA meeting at times when no meeting was scheduled—to visit, find someone, ask questions?
       ____No (Go to question 13)   ____Yes
       If yes:
    b. On the average, how many times each week have you done that?__

13. Do you have an AA sponsor assigned to you at the present time?
    ____No   ____Yes

Scoring Key

Total score was derived by summing the weights for the following items:

Item	Item content	Responses	Weight
1A	Whom do you live with?	Alone	0
		With someone	1
1B	Where do you live?	Other	0
		Rented room	1
		Rented apt.	2
		Own home	3
		Missing	4
02	Number of moves since we last saw you	3+ moves	0
		2 moves	1
		0 or 1 move	2
		3 or more moves	3

Total score was derived by summing the weights for the following items:

Item	Item content	Responses	Weight
04	Total score for eating meals	No meals with others	0
		1 meal	1
		2+ meals	2
		Missing	3
05	Number of different places you have spent the night	6+	0
		5 places	1
		4	2
		3	3
		2	4
		0 or 1	5
06	Number of close friends	None	0
		1 or more	1
07	Number of friends talked with in last week	None	0
		1 or more	1
08	Number of friends you sought out in last week	None	0
		1 or more	1
09	Belong to any organizations except AA	Not in a group	0
		In a group	1
		Officer in group	2
10	Currently in AA	No	0
		Yes	1
12A	Have you gone by AA for visits?	No	0
		Yes	1
13	Currently have AA sponsor	No	0
		Yes	1

EMPLOYMENT

1. a. Are you employed at the present time?
        ____No (Go to question 2)
        ____Yes
    b. Do you work full time or part-time?
        ____Full time   ____Part-time
    c. What hours during the day do you usually work? _____
    d. What days of the week do you usually work? _____
                    (Go to question 3)
2. a. What type of job did you last have? _____
    b. How long ago did you leave the job? _____
    c. Under what circumstances did you leave the job?
        ____Quit   ____Fired   ____Retired
        ____Laid off   ____Disabled   ____Other
    d. Have you looked for other work? ____No   ____Yes

3. a. What type of job is it? _____
    b. How much do you earn? Per year _____ Per month _____
        Per week _____   (Hollingshead #_____)
                                    ____1 $0–50 per week, or presently
                                           unemployed
                                    ____2 $51–100
                                    ____3 $101–150
                                    ____4 $151–200
                                    ____5 $201–250
                                    ____6 $251+
    c. Do you receive room and/or board as payment for work?
        ____No   ____Yes   ____Unemployed
    d. Are you self-employed?
        ____No   ____Yes
    e. Is the work temporary or permanent?
        ____Temporary   ____Permanent   ____Unemployed
    f. Is the work steady or seasonal?
        ____Steady   ____Seasonal
4. How long have you had/did you have this job?
    ____Unemployed   ____6–12 months
    ____<3 months   ____1–2 years
    ____3–6 months   ____2 years +
5. a. In the last 3 months (or since we last saw you) have you missed
        work for any reasons when you were supposed to be there?
        ____No (Go to question 6)   ____Yes
        If Yes:
    b. How many days? ____
    c. How long ago was the last time? ____
    d. How many of these lost days were due to drinking in any form?
        ____0 days   ____6–9
        ____1–2   ____10 or more
        ____3–5   ____Not applicable
6. In the past 3 months (or since we last saw you) have you received a
    pay raise on the job?
    ____No   ____Yes
7. In the past 3 months (or since we last saw you) have you received any
    kind of promotion on the job?
    ____No   ____Yes
8. In the past 3 months (or since we last saw you) how many jobs have
    you held (consecutively or concurrently)?
    ____None (Go to question 10)   ____One   ____More than one
                                               (How many? ____)

9. In the past 3 months (or since we last saw you) how many jobs have you left because of drinking?
    ____None   ____One or more
10. a. What was the best job you ever had? _____
    b. How much did you make? _____
        ____per year
        ____per month
        ____per week
        ____Hollingshead #

Scoring Key

Total score was derived by summing the weights for the following items:

Item	Item content	Responses	Weight
1A	Current employment	No job	0
		Part-time job	1
		Full-time job	2
3B	Amount earned per week	Unemployed	0
		$0–50	1
		$51–100	2
		$101–150	3
		$151–200	4
		$201–250	5
		$251+	6
04	How long have you had this job?	Unemployed	0
		Employed	1
		Less than 3 months	2
		3–6 months	3
		6–12 months	4
		1–2 years	5
		2 years +	6
05	Days missed due to drinking	Not employed	0
		10+ days	1
		6–9 days	2
		3–5 days	3
		2–3 days	4
		0 days	5
06	Received a pay raise	No	0
		Yes	1
07	Received a promotion	No	0
		Yes	1
09	Number of jobs left because of drinking	1 or more	0
		None	1

ECONOMIC

1. a. How much money do you spend per month for rent and/or pay-
        ments for where you live?
        ____$0 (Go to question 1d)
        ____$1–49
        ____$50–74
        ____$75–99
        ____$100
    b. Does that money go toward rent or purchase?
        ____Rent (Go to question 2)   ____Purchase
        If purchase:
    c. How much do you owe at the present time? ____(Go to question 2)
    d. Do you own your own home?
        ____No   ____Yes
2. a. Do you have a savings account that is in your name?
        ____No (Go to question 3)   ____Yes
        If yes:
    b. How long have you had this one? _____
    c. How much is in it? _____
3. a. Do you have a checking account that is in your name?
        ____No (Go to question 4)   ____Yes
        If yes:
    b. How long have you had this one? _____
    c. How many times have you overdrawn it in the past 3 months (or
        since we last saw you)?
        ____0 times   ____1 or more times
4. a. Do you have a car that is in your name?
        ____No (Go to question 5)   ____Yes
        If yes:
    b. Are you making payments or do you own it clear?
        ____Own it clear (Go to question 5)
        ____Making payments
    c. How much do you owe? _____
    d. How long have you been making payments? _____
5. In the past 3 months (or since we last saw you) have you received any
    other financial assistance from any source (such as public welfare, job
    taining scholarships, food stamps)?
    ____No   ____Yes
    If yes:
    From whom? _____
6. a. In the past 3 months (or since we last saw you) have you bought
        anything you would consider expensive?
        ____No (Go to question 7)   ____Yes

7. How many credit cards or charge accounts do you have?
    ____None   ____One or more
8. In the past 3 months (or since we last saw you) have you fallen behind
    in paying your bills?
    ____No   ____Yes

Scoring Key

Total score was derived by summing the weights for the following items:

Item	Item content	Responses	Weight
1A	Amount per month for housing	Missing	0
		$0	1
		$1–49	2
		$50–74	3
		$75–99	4
		$100 and over	5
		Own home	6
2C	Amount in savings	No savings account	0
		Less than $100	1
		$100–500	2
		$501–1000	3
		More than $1000	4
3A	Checking account	No checking account	0
		Checking overdrawn	1
		Checking not overdrawn	2
4A	Own a car	Do not own a car	0
		Making payments on a car	1
		Own car—no payments	2
05	Any welfare recently?	Yes	0
		No	1
07	Number of credit cards	None	0
		One or more	1
08	Fallen behind paying bills in last 3 months	Yes	0
		No	1

LEGAL

1. a. In the past 3 months (or since we last saw you) have you been picked up by the police at all, regardless of whether you went to jail or were guilty of anything?
   ____No (Go to question 2)   ____Yes
   b. How many times:
   ____0 times   ____1 time   ____2 or more times
   c. On what charges (or for what reason)?_____

2. a. In the past 3 months (or since we last saw you) have you spent any time in jail?
   ____No (Go to question 3)   ____Yes
   If yes:
   b. How many times?
   ____0 times   ____1 time   ____2 or more times

3. a. In the past 3 months (or since we last saw you) have you had a court appearance?
   ____No (Go to question 5)   ____Yes
   If yes:
   b. How many times?
   ____0 times   ____1 time   ____2 or more times

4. a. Have you been found guilty in any of the court appearances?
   ____No (Go to question 5)   ____Yes
   If yes:
   b. How many times?
   ____0 times   ____1 time   ____2 or more times
   c. What were the charges? _____

5. a. Are you on probation or parole at this time?
   ____No (Go to question 6)   ____Yes
   b. For how long were you sentenced? _____
   c. How much time remains to go?_____
   d. What were the charges? _____

6. a. In the past 3 months (or since we last saw you) have you been in any alcoholic treatment facility, county hospital, psychiatric hospital, prison, or reform school (excluding jail terms noted above)?
   ____No (Go to question 7)   ____Yes
   b. Which one? _____
   c. From what date(s) to what date(s)? _____
   d. Under what charges or conditions? _____

7. a. In the past 3 months (or since we last saw you) have you received any traffic tickets (excluding parking tickets)?
   ____No (Go to question 8)   ____Yes
   If yes:

b.   How many altogether?
    ____0 times   ____1 time   ____2 or more times
c.   How many were moving violations? _____
d.   How many violations involved drinking in any way? _____
8. a. In the past 3 months (or since we last saw you) have any driving-under-the-influence charges been brought against you?
    ____No (Go to question 9)   ____Yes
    If yes:
   b. How many?
    ____0 times   ____1 time   ____2 or more times
9.   Do you have a driver's license? ____No   ____Yes
10. Have you had a driver's license revoked (or suspended) in the past 3 months (or since we last saw you)?
    ____No   ____Yes
11. a. Are there any charges now pending against you (other than those already noted here)? ____No   ____Yes
    If yes:
    b. What are they? _____

Scoring Key

Total score was derived by summing the weights for the following items:

Item	Item content	Responses	Weight
1B	How many times arrested	Missing	0
		0 times	1
		1 time	2
		2 or more	3
2B	How many times in jail?	Missing	0
		0 times	1
		1 time	2
		2 or more	3
3B	Number of court appearances	Missing	0
		0 times	1
		1 time	2
		2 or more	3
4B	Number of times guilty	Missing	0
		0 times	1
		1 time	2
		2 or more	3
5A	On probation or parole?	No	0
		Yes	1
6A	Been in any alcoholic treatment center	No	0
		Yes	1
7B	Number of tickets	Missing	0
		0 tickets	1

Total score was derived by summing the weights for the following items:

Item	Item content	Responses	Weight
		1 ticket	2
		2 or more	3
8B	How many DWIs?	Missing	0
		0 times	1
		1 time	2
		2 or more	3
09	Have driver's license?	Yes	0
		No	1
10	License been revoked or suspended?	No	0
		Yes	1

appendix L
BEHAVIOR RATING SCALE—DRINKING

INSTRUCTIONS

At first, converse with the S in a general way about drinking. How have things been going? Have you been drinking at all? Have you been completely abstinent? With these general notions, then go to the specific questions.

1. In the last 3 months (or since we last saw you) have you drunk any alcoholic beverages at all?
    ____No (Implies complete abstinence) (Go to question 2)
    ____Yes (Go to question 4)
2. What is the one main reason you have stayed abstinent?
    ____I am not so worried, depressed, or anxious.
    ____I have more responsibilities to think about.
    ____I have fewer responsibilities to think about.
    ____I don't like the bad effects liquor has on me.
    ____Other (Specify) _____
    ____Don't know
3. How much do you miss drinking?
    1   Not at all
    2   Very little
    3   Some moderate amount
    4   A lot
    5   Very much (a great deal)
    (Go to question 13)
4. a. Have you been drinking *more* in the last 3 months (or since we last saw you) than you were in the previous comparable time period?
        ____No (Go to question 5)   ____Yes
        If yes:
    b. What is the one main reason you have been drinking more lately?
        ____I am more worried, anxious, or depressed.
        ____I have more responsibilities to think about.
        ____I have fewer responsibilities to think about.
        ____I enjoy drinking more.
        ____Other (Specify) _____
        ____Don't know.
        (Go to question 7)
5. a. Was/were there any period(s) of time in the last 3 months (or since we last saw you) when you didn't have any alcohol to drink for more than 1 day at a time? (Dry)
        ____No (Go to question 6)   ____Yes
        If yes:

   b. About how many times have you done this in the last 3 months (or since we last saw you)? _____
   c. From what date(s) to what date(s)? _____
   d. What was the main factor associated with your stopping drinking and becoming dry at that time?
       ___Became too sick to go on (or passed out).
       ___Someone else forced me to stop.
       ___Ran out of money.
       ___I no longer felt a need to keep drinking.
       ___I decided to stop.
       ___Other (explain) _____
       ___Don't know.
6. In the last 3 months (or since we last saw you), how often have you stopped after taking one or two drinks?
    1 Never
    2 Very few times
    3 Sometimes
    4 Many times

The next few questions will ask you about your use of various types of drinks, i.e., wine, beer, and hard liquor.

Please tell me how often you usually have had (*beverage*) in the last 3 months (or since we last saw you).

	(7.) Wine	(8.) Beer	(9.) Liquor (hard)
3 or more times/day			
2/day			
1/day			
Nearly every day			
3–4/week			
1–2/week			
2–3/week			
about 1/month			
Less than 1/month; but at least 1/3 months			
Never			

(Any beverage that is never drunk should be deleted from questions 10, 11, and 12.)

A. Think of all the times you have had (*beverage*) in the last 3 months (or since we last saw you). When you have drunk (*beverage*) recently how often have you had 1 or 2 or 3 (*measure[s]*)? (Measures = glasses for wine; cans or glasses for beer; drinks or shots for hard liquor.)

		10.	11.	12.
				Hard
		Wine	Beer	liquor
a.	Nearly every time			
b.	Often; more than half the time			
c.	Sometimes; less than half the time			
d.	Once in a while			
e.	Never			

B.   When you have drunk (*beverage*) recently, how often have you had 4 or 5 or 6 (*measure[s]*)?

		Wine	Beer	Hard liquor
a.	Nearly every time			
b.	Often; more than half the time			
c.	Sometimes; less than half the time			
d.	Once in a while			
e.	Never			

C.   When you have drunk (*beverage*) recently, how often have you had 7 or more (*measure[s]*)?

		Wine	Beer	Hard liquor
a.	Nearly every time			
b.	Often; more than half the time			
c.	Sometimes; less than half the time			
d.	Once in a while			
e.	Never			

13.   a.   Do you smoke at the present time?
　　　　　____No (Go to question 14)
　　　　　____Yes   ____Cigarettes   ____Cigars   ____Pipe

14.   a.   In the past 3 months (or since we last saw each other) have you used any alcoholic substitutes (such as canned heat, shaving lotion, hair tonic)?
　　　　　____No (Go to question 15)   ____Yes, once
　　　　　____Yes, several times

If yes:

　　b.   Once you started using such a substitute, how many cans or bottles did you drink per day? ____ Per week? ____

　　c.   Once you started, how long did you go on drinking it? _____

15. In the past 3 months (or since we last saw you) have you used any drugs or medication, such as sleeping pills, pep pills, tranquilizers, reefers, narcotics, hallucinogens, in an abusive manner?

    ____No   ____Yes (Explain) _____

16. Do you want to be able to have 2 or 3 drinks and be able to stop?

    ____No   ____Yes   ____Don't know

17. Do you think there will be a time when you can have 2 or 3 drinks and stop?

    ____No   ____Yes   ____Don't know

18. Do you want to stop drinking completely?

    ____No   ____Yes   ____Don't know

19. Do you think there will be a time when you will stop drinking completely for good?

    ____No   ____Yes   ____Don't know

20. a. Are you presently taking any medications? ____No (Go to question 21)

    ____Yes   What is it? _____

    b. What are you taking it for?

    ____Control my drinking

    ____Relieve symptoms of drinking

    ____Alleviate nervousness

    ____Other (Explain) _____

    ____Don't know

21. I have here some reasons that various other people have said were reasons for their drinking. I'll read these and I would like to have you tell me how important each one was to *you* as a reason why you drank in the last 3 months (or since we last saw you). I'm not interested in the effect alcohol had on you, or how it made you feel, but rather why you might have had the first drink, or why you might have continued to drink.

		1 Very important	2 Fairly important	3 Not at all important
a.	I drank because it helped me to relax	2	1	0
b.	I drank to be sociable	X	X	X
c.	I liked the taste	X	X	X
d.	I drank because the people I knew drank	X	X	X
e.	I drank when I wanted to forget everything	2	1	0
f.	I drank to celebrate special occasions	X	X	X
g.	A drink helped me to forget my worries	2	1	0
h.	A small drink improved my appetite for food	X	X	X
i.	I accepted a drink because it was the polite thing to do in certain situations	X	X	X

j.	A drink helped cheer me up when I was in a bad mood	2	1	0
k.	I drank because I needed it when I was tense and nervous	2	1	0
l.	I drank because it helped me to work better	X	X	X
m.	A drink helped me to be more alert mentally	X	X	X
n.	I drank because it helped me to feel superior	X	X	X

22. Are there any other reasons you can think of why you start or continue drinking?

appendix M
DRINKING
CLASSIFICATION INDICES

COMPUTATION OF ETHANOL INTAKE FROM Q-F-V SCALES

Using quantity-frequency-variability (Q-F-V) scales of alcohol consumption similar to those originally developed by Calahan, Cissin, and Crossley (1969), a rough estimate of the respondent's average ethanol intake per day can be made. The Q-F-V instrument consists of two scales: 1) A frequency scale, designed to determine how often the respondent drinks each of three types of alcohol (beer, wine, and liquor). The scale range is from "three times a day" to "never" and each scale point may be converted to a proportion of the total time span considered (F) (see Table M-5). 2) The quantity-variability scale. Quantities are expressed in units frequently used with the specific alcohol beverage considered (e.g., 12-oz. bottles of beer, 4-oz. glasses of wine, and 1-oz. shots of liquor). For each of three quantity ranges ("7 or more," "3, 4, or 5," "1, 2, or 3") the respondent indicates how often he drinks that quantity of beverage. That is, are seven or more shots of liquor consumed "every time," "often," "sometimes," "once in a while," or "never"? Thus both quantity and variability of consumption are estimated.

With the information obtained in the quantity-variability scale, ounces of alcohol consumed per drinking occasion can be estimated. The median quantity listed is multiplied by the unit used for each type of alcohol. Table M-1 lists the quantity (Q) obtained from the computation.

Because drinking is variable, each of the quantities listed in Table M-1 may be consumed some proportion of the time (P). Table M-4 may be used to compute the proportion (see also Calahan et al., 1969, p. 214). A summation of each quantity times its proportion provides an estimate of the ounces of each beverage consumed per drinking occasion (Bev/oz). In other words:

$$\text{Bev/oz} = QP \tag{1}$$

Total ethanol intake per drinking occasion (ethanol total) can be determined by multiplying the ounces for each beverage (Bev/oz) with a special proportion of ethanol (P_E) contained in that beverage and summing these products. Thus it is assumed that beer is 4% ethanol, wine is 15%, and liquor is 45%. These proportions are consistent with those used by Armor, Polich, and Stambul (1978) and by Calahan et al. (1969). In other words:

$$\text{Ethanol total} = (\text{Beer/oz} \times 0.04) + (\text{Wine/oz} \times 0.15) + (\text{Liquor/oz} \times 0.45) \tag{2}$$

Finally, an estimate of the average ethanol intake per day can be made by multiplying the frequency (F) of each beverage times Bev/oz times the ethanol constant for that beverage and summing those products, i.e.:

$$\text{Ethanol per day} = (F \text{ beer} \times \text{beer/oz} \times 0.04) + (F \text{ wine} \times \text{wine/oz} \times 0.15) + (F \text{ liquor} \times \text{liquor/oz} \times 0.45) \tag{3}$$

Table M-1.   Ounces of beverage consumed for each
level of the quantity-variability scale

Quantity scale	Median quantity	12 oz beer	4 oz wine
7 or more	8	96	32
4, 5, or 6	5	60	20
1, 2, or 3	2	24	8

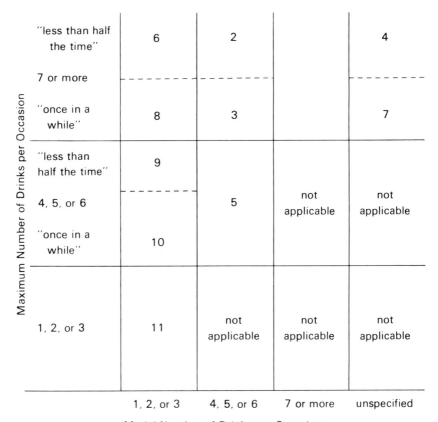

Figure M-1.   Quantity-variability (Q-V) classifications of the Q-F-V index. (Modified—for
original classification, see Calahan et al., 1969, p. 13.)

Table M-2.   Quantity-variability classifications

Quantity-variability class	Modal quantity (amount drunk "nearly every time" or "more than half the time")	Maximum quantity (highest quantity drunk)
1	7 or more	7 or more
2	4, 5, or 6	7 or more "less than half the time"
3	4, 5, or 6	7 or more "once in a while"
4	No mode specified	7 or more "less than half the time"
5	4, 5, or 6	4, 5, or 6
6	1, 2, or 3	7 or more "less than half the time"
7	No mode specified	7 or more "once in a while"
8	1, 2, or 3	7 or more "once in a while"
9	1, 2, or 3	3, 4, or 5 "less than half the time"
10	1, 2, or 3	3, 4, or 5 "once in a while"
11	1, 2, or 3	1, 2, or 3

Modified—for original classification see: Calahan, D., Cisin, I. H., Crossly, H. M. 1969. *American Drinking Practices: A National Survey of Drinking Behavior and Attitudes*, p. 13. Rutgers Center of Alcohol Studies, New Brunswick, N.J.

Table M-3.   Q-F-V classifications

Q-F-V group	Frequency (of any alcoholic beverage)		Quantity-variability class (beverage drunk most often)	Classi-fication codes
1. Heavy drinkers	a.	3 or more times a day	1–11	1
	b.	'2 times a day	1–9	
	c.	Every day or nearly every day	1–8	
	d.	3 or 4 times a week	1–5	
	e.	1 or 2 times a week	1–4	
	f.	2 or 3 times a month	1	
2. Moderate drinkers	a.	2 times a day	10–11	2
	b.	Every day or nearly every day	9–10	
	c.	3 or 4 times a week	6–9	
	d.	1 or 2 times a week	5–9	
	e.	2 or 3 times a month	2–8	
	f.	About once a month	1–6	
3. Light drinkers	a.	Every day or nearly every day	11	3
	b.	1 to 4 times a week	10–11	
	c.	2 or 3 times a month	9–11	
	d.	About once a month	7–11	
4. Infrequent drinkers		Drank less than once a month but at least once every 3 months[a]		4
5. Abstainers		Drank none of the 3 beverages (never)[b]		5

[a] Modified: Original statement from Calahan et al. is: Drank less than once a month but at least once a year.

[b] Modified: Original statement from Calahan et al. is: Drank none of the three beverages as often as once or never.

Table M-4.   Proportion of drinking per occasion computation

For each beverage (wine, beer, liquor) the proportion of time that the subject spent consuming is calculated using the information given in the BRS Drinking Questionnaire. Please note the order of the information requested.

Part I.   7 or more measures of beverage

Where Weight checked

a. Nearly every time
b. Often; more than half the time
c. Sometimes; less than half the time
d. Once in a while
e. Never

Weight	checked
4	
3	
2	
1	
0	

Weight checked _____ for 7 or more measures   (C)

Part II.   3, 4, or 5 measures of beverage

Where Weight checked

a. Nearly every time
b. Often; more than half the time
c. Sometimes; less than half the time
d. Once in a while
e. Never

Weight	checked
4	
3	
2	
1	
0	

Weight checked _____ for 3, 4, or 5 measures   (B)

Part III.   1, 2, or 3 measures of beverage

Where Weight checked

a. Nearly every time
b. Often; more than half the time
c. Sometimes; less than half the time
d. Once in a while
e. Never

Weight	checked
4	
3	
2	
1	
0	

Weight checked _____ for 1, 2, or 3 measures   (A)

Total of all weights checked _____ (Cannot be greater than 6)

Parts[a]	Measures[a]	Weight checked	÷	Total of all weights	=	Proportion of Occasion for beverage[b]
III	1, 2, or 3	___(A) ÷		_____	=	0.___(A)
II	4, 5, or 6	___(B) ÷		_____	=	0.___(B)
I	7 or 8	___(C) ÷		_____	=	0.___(C)

[a] Note the reversal of the Parts and Measures.

[b] When the three proportions are added together they must equal 1.00; if they do not you have made an arithmetic error.

Note:
Part I.
1. Code directly from appropriate beverage information, e.g., question 10C for wine, 13C for Beer, and 12C for liquor in the Behavior Ratio Scale (Drinking).

Part II.
1. If you checked (a) (Nearly every time) in Part I then you must check (3) (Never) in Part II.
2. If you checked (b) (Often; more than half the time) in Part I then you must check (c) (Sometimes; less than half the time) in Part II.
3. If you checked (c) (Sometimes; less than half the time) in Part I you *can't* check (a) (Nearly every time) in Part II—check (b) (Often; more than half the time) instead.

Part III.
1. If you checked (a) (Nearly every time) in Part I then you must check (e) (Never) in Part III.
2. If you checked (b) (Often; more than half the time) in Part I then you must check (e) (Never) in Part III.
3. If you checked (a) (Nearly every time) in Part II then you must check (e) (Never) in Part III.
4. If you checked (b) (Often; more than half the time) in Part II and you checked (c) (Sometimes; less than half the time) in Part I then you must check (e) (Never) in Part III.
5. If you checked (d) (once in a while) in both Parts I and II then you must check (a) (Nearly every time) in Part III.
6. If you do not drink this beverage at all you must check (e) (Never) in Parts I, II, and III.
7. If you checked (e) (Never) in Part I and either (d) (Once in a while) or (e) (Never) in Part II and note 6 does not apply, then you must check (a) (Nearly every time) in Part III.

Table M-5.   Frequency of consumption (for the volume-variability index)

How often you usually drink a beverage[a] (wine, beer, hard liquor)	Number of drinking occasions per 90 days	Number of drinking occasions per day
3 or more times/day	270	3.000
2/day	180	2.000
1/day	90	1.000
Nearly every day	66	0.733
3–4/week	45	0.500
1–2/week	21	0.233
2–3/month	7.5	0.083
About 1/month	3	0.033
Less than 1/month but at least 1/3 months[b]	1.5[d]	0.017
Never[c]	0	0.000

Modified for 90 days instead of 1 month. For original see: Calahan, D., Cisin, I. H., Crossly, H. M. 1969. *American Drinking Practices: A National Survey of Drinking Behavior and Attitudes*, pp. 213–214. Rutgers Center of Alcohol Studies, New Brunswick, N.J.

[a] See BRS—Drinking for responses.

[b] Modified: Original statement from Calahan et al. is: Less than once a month but at least once a year.

[c] Modified: Original statement from Calahan et al. is: Less than once a year or never.

[d] No value was assigned to this category and persons were not asked the amount and variability of consumption in the Calahan et al. study. This is *not* the case in this study (see also note [c]).

Table M-6.   Average number of drinks of a beverage per day

For each beverage (wine, beer, and liquor) use the following procedure to calculate the average number of drinks (wine = 4-oz glass; beer = 12-oz glass bottles; liquor = 1-oz shots) that a client used per day over a 90-day period under investigation.

Part A.   Total drinks by measure

Beverage = ⎯⎯⎯⎯⎯⎯

Measure	Proportion of occasion for beverage[a]	×	Average number of drinks	=	Total drinks by measure
1, 2, or 3	0.___(A)	×	2	=	⎯⎯⎯⎯
4, 5, or 6	0.___(B)	×	5	=	⎯⎯⎯⎯
7 or more	0.___(C)	×	8	=	⎯⎯⎯⎯

Part B.   Total drinks by occasion

Total drinks by measure 1, 2, or 3	+	Total drinks by measure 3, 4, or 5	+	Total drinks by measure, 7 or more	=	Total drinks by occasion
⎯⎯⎯⎯	+	⎯⎯⎯⎯	+	⎯⎯⎯⎯	=	⎯⎯⎯⎯

Part C.   Average drinks of beverage per day

Total drinks by occasion	×	Frequency of consumption (occasions per day)[b]	=	Average drinks per day
⎯⎯⎯⎯	×	⎯⎯⎯⎯	=	⎯⎯⎯⎯

See: Calahan, D., Cisin, I. H., Crossly, H. M. 1969. *American Drinking Practices: A National Survey of Drinking Behavior and Attitudes*, pp. 213–215. Rutgers Center of Alcohol Studies, New Brunswick, N.J.

[a] See Appendix M, Table M-4.

[b] See Table M-5 (which converts responses of the appropriate beverage frequency question Q9W, Q10B, Q11L) to occasion per day.

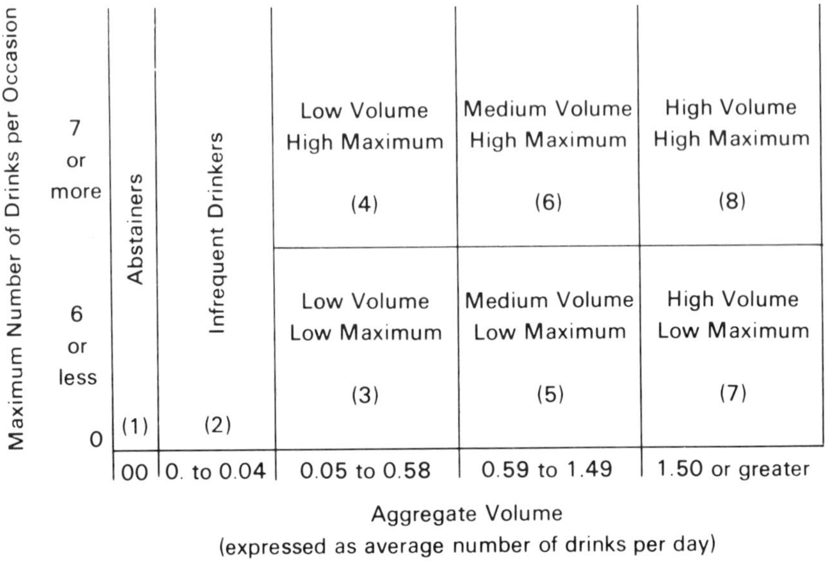

Figure M-2.   Volume-variability (V-V) index. (1) Abstainers: Those who drank less than once a year or never. (2) Infrequent Drinkers: Those who drank at least once in 3 months. (Modified—high maximum went from 5 or more to 7 or more. For original classification see Calahan et al., 1969, pp. 213–214.)

appendix N
THERAPIST
EVALUATION FORM

Therapists: Please rate patients on a scale from 1 to 5, at close of therapy.
             The following areas will be covered:
             A.   Social Relationships
             B.   Employment
             C.   Economic
             D.   Legal
             E.   Drinking

1.   Social Relationships
   a.   Good relationships with significant others (Check one)
      1   ____Poor
      2   ____Fair
      3   ____Medium
      4   ____Good
      5   ____Excellent
   b.   Relatively permanent residence
      1   ____Poor
      2   ____Fair
      3   ____Medium
      4   ____Good
      5   ____Excellent
   c.   Involvement in at least one community activity (other than drinking)
      1   ____Poor
      2   ____Fair
      3   ____Medium
      4   ____Good
      5   ____Excellent
   Comments (if any)

2.   Employment
   a.   Steady source of income
      1   ____Poor
      2   ____Fair
      3   ____Medium
      4   ____Good
      5   ____Excellent
   b.   Utilizes his skills, or is in process of acquiring some
      1   ____Poor
      2   ____Fair
      3   ____Medium
      4   ____Good
      5   ____Excellent

   c. Is free from a tendency to make frequent moves from occupation to occupation or job to job (with the exception of moves to better jobs or more meaningful life experience)

     1 ____Poor
     2 ____Fair
     3 ____Medium
     4 ____Good
     5 ____Excellent
     Comments (if any)

3. Economic

   a. Meets his financial obligations

     1 ____Poor
     2 ____Fair
     3 ____Medium
     4 ____Good
     5 ____Excellent

   b. Takes a realistic view of allocating his funds

     1 ____Poor
     2 ____Fair
     3 ____Medium
     4 ____Good
     5 ____Excellent

   c. Copes with his financial situation without undue worry and strain

     1 ____Poor
     2 ____Fair
     3 ____Medium
     4 ____Good
     5 ____Excellent
     Comments (if any)

4. Legal

   a. Arrest history

     1 ____Poor
     2 ____Fair
     3 ____Medium
     4 ____Good
     5 ____Excellent (None)

   b. Time spent in jail

     1 ____Poor
     2 ____Fair
     3 ____Medium
     4 ____Good
     5 ____Excellent (None)

    c. Traffic violations

       1 ____Poor

       2 ____Fair

       3 ____Medium

       4 ____Good

       5 ____Excellent (None)

       Comments (if any)

5. Drinking

    a. Freedom from alcohol-related health problems

       1 ____Poor

       2 ____Fair

       3 ____Medium

       4 ____Good

       5 ____Excellent

    b. Freedom from alcohol-related social (including family) problems

       1 ____Poor

       2 ____Fair

       3 ____Medium

       4 ____Good

       5 ____Excellent

    c. Freedom from alcohol-related employment problems

       1 ____Poor

       2 ____Fair

       3 ____Medium

       4 ____Good

       5 ____Excellent

       Comments (if any)

6. Has the patient's major complaint been resolved?

    Comments:

7. Have problematic attitudes related to this area improved?

    Comments:

appendix O
STATISTICAL TABLES FOR ACCEPTED VS. REJECTED CLIENTS

Table O-1.   Means and standard deviations from accepted and rejected clients on reported drinking behavior

Variable	Accepted (N = 247)	Rejected (N = 150)	t(395)
Ounces of ethanol usually consumed	14.41	16.13	−1.36
(SD)	(11.79)	(12.97)	
Major physiological index	5.04	4.11	2.82[a]
(SD)	(3.11)	(3.39)	
Major behavioral and attitudinal index	3.63	3.28	2.75[a]
(SD)	(1.17)	(1.30)	
Minor behavioral and attitudinal index	3.80	3.09	3.99[b]
(SD)	(1.66)	(1.80)	
Total drinking index	12.47	10.47	3.84[b]
	(4.68)	(5.57)	

[a] $p < 0.01$.
[b] $p < 0.001$.

Table O-2.   Means and standard deviations for completing the Trail Making Test

	Accepted	Rejected	t^a
Trails A[b]	34.90	63.62	−12.36[c]
(SD)	(8.75)	(32.18)	
Trails B[d]	82.84	140.31	−9.74
(SD)	(31.97)	(66.58)	

[a] Because of unequal variances an approximation for t was computed (SPSS, 1976).
[b] $N = 261$ and 203; df = 225.
[c] $p < 0.001$.
[d] $N = 255$ and 144; df = 181.

Table O-3.   Means and standard deviations for IQ scores

Variable	Accepted (N = 262)	Rejected (N = 218)	t(478)
Kent EGY Score	29.15	22.48	13.31[a]
(SD)	(4.44)	(6.48)	
Conversion IQ	91.81	78.56	13.07[a]
(SD)	(7.74)	(14.04)	

[a] $p < 0.001$.

Table O-4.   Means and standard deviations for age
and education at time of screening

Variable	Accepted (N = 262)	Rejected (N = 226)	t(486)
Age	39.69	42.67	-3.76^a
(SD)	(7.82)	(9.67)	
Education	10.15	7.53	9.37^a
(SD)	(2.96)	(3.20)	

[a] $p < 0.01.$

Table O-5.   Contingency table for employment
status, marital status, and reading ability

Variable	Accepted	Rejected	χ^2
Employed			
Yes	181	131	5.74^a
No	81	94	
Married			
Yes	104	65	5.93^a
No	158	161	
Reads[b]			
Yes	163	57	40.95^c
No	34	62	

[a] $p < 0.05.$

[b] Defined as reading better than a sixth grade level.

[c] $p < 0.001.$

Table O-6.   Contingency tables for the subjective[a] and objective[b] assessment of mental status

	Accepted	Rejected	$\chi^{2\,c}$
Subjective[d]			
Delusions			
Present	4	10	2.93
Absent	241	194	
Hallucinations			
Present	5	12	3.52
Absent	240	192	
Recent Memory			
Not impaired	205	132	22.55[e]
Mild impairment	39	60	
Severe impairment	1	9	
Remote memory			
Not impaired	213	131	32.11[e]
Mild impairment	31	55	
Severe impairment	1	13	
Objective			
Delusions			
Present	52	54	1.05
Absent	210	170	
Hallucinations			
Present	40	44	1.27
Absent	222	181	
Recent Memory			
Not impaired	140	115	<1
Mild impairment	96	82	
Severe impairment	26	27	
Remote Memory			
Not impaired	232	126	67.23[e]
Mild impairment	30	93	
Severe impairment	0	6	

[a] Social worker ratings of client's mental status.

[b] Assessment based on analysis of responses recorded for the client with questions in the interview.

[c] Degrees of freedom for 2 × 2 tables are 1; for 3 × 2 tables are 2.

[d] Total N may differ from variable to variable because of missing data.

[e] $p < 0.001$.

Table O-7.   Assessment of brain functioning based on an impairment index computed from Trail Making performances

	Accepted	Rejected	χ^2 (1)
Impaired			
Yes	69	186	171.98[a]
No	189	26	
Total[b]	258	212	

[a] $p < 0.001$.

[b] Variation in N due to missing data. Variable is based on a computed score.

appendix P
DROPOUTS VS. COMPLETORS ON SCREENING AND DRINKING QUESTIONNAIRES

Table P-1.   Comparisons—dropouts vs. completers

Variable	Dropout (≤9 = 0)	(N)	Complete (≥10)	(N)	df	F value	p
Weight of individual	156.40	(20)	159.25	(73)	91	1.45	—
SD	21.66		26.09				
Tremors	1.18	(143)	1.24	(104)	245	1.23	—
SD	0.39		0.43				
Seizures	1.81	(143)	1.86	(104)	245	1.24	—
SD	0.39		0.35				
Hallucinations	1.66	(143)	1.75	(104)	245	1.20	—
SD	0.48		0.44				
DTs	1.72	(143)	1.77	(104)	245	1.13	—
SD	0.45		0.42				
Ethyl alcohol consumed via beer	3.59	(143)	4.62	(104)	245	1.81	0.001
SD	4.22		5.67				
Ethyl alcohol consumed via wine	2.73	(143)	3.87	(104)	245	2.03	0.001
SD	6.33		9.01				
Ethyl alcohol consumed via liquor	7.76	(143)	6.41	(104)	245	1.68	0.009
SD	8.13		6.37				
Total ounces consumed via beer, wine, liquor	14.05	(143)	14.90	(104)	245	1.38	0.074
SD	10.96		12.89				
Total consumption of alcohol over minimum	1.34	(143)	1.40	(104)	245	1.07	—
SD	0.48		0.49				
Drinks for more than 1 day in a row	1.04	(139)	1.07	(104)	241	1.81	0.005
SD	0.19		0.25				
Have you had blackouts while drinking?	1.26	(141)	1.24	(104)	243	1.04	—
SD	0.44		0.43				
Does the doctor advise no drink?	1.39	(115)	1.38	(90)	203	1.01	—
SD	0.49		0.49				
Have you lost a job because of drinking?	1.51	(142)	1.56	(104)	244	1.01	—
SD	0.50		0.50				
Had marriage problems because of drinking?	1.31	(143)	1.41	(101)	242	1.12	—
SD	0.47		0.49				
Arrested for any alcohol-related offenses?	1.06	(143)	1.07	(104)	245	1.19	—
SD	0.12		0.17				
Lost job or marriage problem or arrested?	1.01	(143)	1.03	(104)	245	2.04	0.001
SD	0.12		0.17				
Can you stop drinking after two drinks?	1.67	(143)	1.62	(1)	245	1.08	—
SD	0.47		0.49				

Table P-1. *Continued*

Variable	Dropout ($\leq 9 = 0$)	(N)	Complete (≥ 10)	(N)	df	F value	p
Do you hide your drinking?	1.35	(116)	1.42	(88)	202	1.07	—
SD	0.48		0.50				
Do you drink in the morning?	1.14	(116)	1.27	(88)	202	1.67	0.010
SD	0.35		0.45				
Have you lost interest in activities?	1.50	(143)	1.60	(103)	244	1.04	—
SD	0.50		0.49				
Have you become angry while drinking?	1.46	(143)	1.57	(103)	244	1.01	—
SD	0.50		0.50				
Wife complains about your drinking?	1.21	(142)	1.22	(101)	241	1.03	—
SD	0.41		0.42				
Do you drink to relieve anger?	1.09	(143)	1.09	(104)	245	1.04	—
SD	0.29		0.28				
Major psychological index	5.28	(143)	4.72	(104)	245	1.03	
SD	3.13		3.08				
Major behavioral, psychological, and attitudinal	3.63	(143)	3.63	(104)	245	1.05	—
SD	1.19		1.16				
Major behavioral, psychological, attitudinal index	3.95	(145)	3.59	(104)	245	1.17	—
SD	1.71		1.58				
Total score	12.85	(143)	11.95	(104)	245	1.20	—
SD	4.84		4.42				
Has subject passed or failed questionnaire?	1.10	(143)	1.16	(104)	245	1.55	0.015
SD	0.30		0.87				
Age in years	39.94	(158)	39.32	(104)	260	1.10	—
SD	7.67		8.06				
Education in years	9.94	(158)	10.46	(104)	260	1.15	—
SD	2.87		3.08				
Raw score on Kent IQ	28.94	(158)	29.46	(104)	260	1.12	—
SD	4.54		4.28				
Pass-fail Kent IQ	1.04	(158)	1.03	(104)	260	1.30	—
SD	0.19		0.17				
IQ conversion of Kent IQ	91.33	(158)	92.55	(104)	260	1.28	—
SD	8.09		7.16				
Time on Trails—Part A	35.03	(158)	34.70	(103)	259	1.18	—
SD	9.04		8.33				
Pass or fail—Part A	1.23	(158)	1.21	(103)	259	1.04	—
SD	0.42		0.41				
Time on Trails—Part B	79.95	(154)	87.25	(101)	253	1.18	—
SD	32.85		30.21				
Pass or fail—Part B	1.21	(156)	1.29	(103)	257	1.24	—
SD	0.41		0.46				

Table P-2.   Comparisons—dropouts vs. completers

Variable	Column	Dropout (≤ 9)	(N)	Complete (≥ 10)	(N)	df	Corrected χ^2	p
Presently employed	Yes	40.5	(106)	28.6	(75)	1	0.53	—
	No	19.8	(52)	11.1	(29)	1	0.53	—
Marital status	Married	21.4	(56)	18.3	(48)	1	2.57	—
	Not married	38.9	(102)	21.4	(36)	1	2.57	—
Leading a complicated score based on Gray test	Reads	46.7	(92)	36.0	(71)	1	0.49	—
	Does not read	11.2	(22)	6.1	(12)	1	0.49	—
Subjects' speech	Intelligible	58.9	(149)	40.7	(103)	1	0.04	—
	Unintelligible	0.4	(1)	0.0	(0)	1	0.04	—
Presence of delusions	Present	1.2	(3)	0.4	(1)	2	0.01	—
	Absent	58.4	(143)	40.0	(98)	2	0.01	—
Presence of hallucinations	Present	0.8	(2)	1.2	(3)	2	0.21	—
	Absent	59.2	(145)	38.8	(95)	2	0.21	—
Presence of memory problems— recent	None	51.0	(125)	32.7	(80)	2	0.21	—
	Mild	8.6	(21)	7.3	(18)	2	0.21	—
	Severe	0.4	(2)	0.0	(0)	2	1.36	—
Presence of memory problems— remote	None	53.5	(131)	33.5	(82)	2	1.36	—
	Mild	6.1	(15)	6.5	(16)	2	2.61	—
	Severe	0.4	(2)	0.0	(0)	2	2.61	—
Objective sign of delusions	Present	4.6	(12)	2.7	(7)	2	2.61	—
	Absent	55.7	(146)	37.0	(97)	2	2.61	—
Objective sign of hallucinations	Present	9.2	(24)	6.5	(17)	1	0.00042	—
	Absent	51.1	(134)	33.2	(82)	1	0.00042	—
Objective sign of memory loss	Absent	34.7	(91)	17.6	(46)	1	0.0061	—
	Mild	21.0	(55)	16.8	(44)	1	0.0061	—
	Severe	4.6	(12)	5.3	(14)	1	0.0061	—
Objective sign of remote memory loss	Absent	53.8	(141)	37.4	(98)	2	5.25	0.07
	Mild	6.1	(16)	2.3	(6)	2	5.25	0.07
	Severe	0.4	(1)	0.0	(2)	2	5.25	0.07
Combined Trails A + B Organicity Score	Not impaired	45.7	(118)	27.5	(71)	2	2.25	—
	Impaired	14.7	(38)	12.0	(31)	2	2.25	—

REFERENCES

Alcoholics Anonymous. 1972. Profile of an AA meeting. AA World Services, Inc., New York.

Anthony, W. A., and Carkhuff, R. R. 1977. The functional professional therapeutic agent. In A. S. Gurman and A. M. Razin (eds.), Effective Psychotherapy: A Handbook of Research, pp. 103–119. Pergamon Press, New York.

, Armor, D. J., Polich, J. M., and Stambul, H. B. 1978. Alcoholism and Treatment. John Wiley & Sons, Inc., New York.

Ayers, J. L., Templer, D. I., Ruff, C. F., and Barthlow, V. L. 1978. Trail making test improvement in abstinent alcoholics. J. Stud. Alc. 39:1627–1629.

Baekeland, F., Lundwall, L., and Kissin, B. 1975. Methods for the treatment of chronic alcoholism: A critical appraisal. In R. Gibbins et al. (eds.), Research Advances in Alcohol and Drug Problems. John Wiley & Sons, Inc., New York.

Bergin, A. E. 1971. The evaluation of therapeutic outcomes. In A. E. Bergin and S. L. Garfield (eds.), Handbook of Psychotherapy and Behavior Change, pp. 217–270, John Wiley & Sons, Inc., New York.

Bergin, A. E., and Lambert, M. J. 1978. The evaluation of therapeutic outcomes. In S. L. Garfield and A. E. Bergin (eds.), Handbook of Psychotherapy and Behavior Change, pp. 139–190. 2nd Ed. John Wiley & Sons, Inc., New York.

Bowen, W. T., and Androes, L. 1968. A follow-up study of 79 alcoholic patients: 1963–1965. Bull. Menninger Clin. 32:26–34.

Bowman, R. S., Stein, L. I., and Newton, J. R. 1975. Measurement and interpretation of drinking behavior. J. Stud. Alc. 36:1154–1172.

Brandsma, J. M. 1972a. Drinking Questionnaire. Unpublished materials, University of Kentucky.

Brandsma, J. M. 1972b. Mental Status Interview. Unpublished materials, University of Kentucky.

Brandsma, J. M. 1972c. Problem Check List. Unpublished materials, University of Kentucky.

Brandsma, J. M. 1975. Science, self-concept and the concept of a fallible human being. Rational Living 10(2):15–17.

Brandsma, J. M. 1976. Toward a more rational AA. Rational Living 11(1):35–37.

Brandsma, J. M., Maultsby, M. C., Welsh, R., and Heller, S. 1977. The court probated alcoholic and outpatient treatment attrition. Br. J. Addict. 72:23–30.

Brown, R. A., Fader, K., and Barber, T. X. 1973. Responsiveness to pain: Stimulus specificity vs. genorality. Psychol. Rec. 23:1–7.

Brown, R. F. 1963. An aftercare program for alcoholics. Crime Delinq. 9:77–83.

Bruun, K. 1963. Outcome of different types of treatment of alcoholics. Quart. J. Stud. Alc. 24:280–288.

Butcher, J. N. 1969. MMPI: Research Developments and Clinical Application. McGraw-Hill Book Co., New York.

C., Bill. 1965. The growth and effectiveness of Alcoholics Anonymous in a southwestern city. Quart. J. Stud. Alc. 26:279–284.

Calahan, D., Cissin, I. H., and Crossley, H. M. 1969. American drinking practices: A national survey of drinking behavior and attitudes. Rutgers Center of Alcohol Studies, Monograph No. 6, New Brunswick, N.J.

Chafetz, M. E. 1962. Alcoholism problems and programs in Hungary, Yugoslavia, Romania, and Bulgaria. New Engl. J. Med. 266:1362–1367.

Chafetz, M. E. 1965. Is compulsory treatment of the alcoholic effective? Northwest Med. 64:932–937.

Chafetz, M. E., and Blane, H. T. 1963. Alcohol-crisis treatment approach and establishment of treatment relations with alcoholics. Psychol. Rep. 12:862.

The chronic drunkenness offender in Connecticut. 1957. III. The rehabilitation experiment evaluated. Connecticut Rev. Alc. 9:1–4.

Clancy, J. 1961. Outpatient treatment of the alcoholic. J. Iowa State Med. Soc. 51:221–226.

Clancy, J., Vanderhoof, E., and Campbell, P. 1967. Evaluation of an oversive technique as a treatment for alcoholism; controlled trial with succinylcholine-induced opnea. Quart. J. Stud. Alc. 28:476–485.

Clancy, J., Vornbrock, R., and Vanderhoof, E. 1965. Treatment of alcoholics; a follow-up study. Dis. Nerv. Syst. 26:551–561.

Clapton, J. R. 1978. Alcholism and the MMPI: A review. J. Stud. Alc. 39:1540–1558.

Colby, K. M. 1951. A Primer for Psychotherapists. Ronald Press, New York.

Coleman, J., and Dumas, R. 1962. Contributions of a nurse in an adult psychiatric clinic: An exploratory project. Ment. Hygiene 46:448–453.

Cooke, G., Wehmer, G., and Gruber, J. 1975. Training paraprofessionals in the treatment of alcoholism: Effects on knowledge, attitudes and therapeutic techniques. J. Stud. Alc. 36:938–948.

Cowen, J. 1954. A six year follow-up of a series of committed alcoholics. Quart. J. Stud. Alc. 15:413–423.

Dahlstrom, W. G., Welsh, G. S., and Dahlstrom, L. E. 1972. An MMPI Handbook: Clinical Interpretations. Minneapolis University Press, Minneapolis.

Davies, D. L., Shepard, M., and Myers, E. 1956. The two years prognosis of fifty alcohol addicts after treatment in a hospital. Quart. J. Stud. Alc. 17:485–502.

Ditman, K., and Cohen, S. 1959. Evaluation of drugs in the treatment of alcoholism. Quart. J. Stud. Alc. 20:573–576.

Ditman, K. S., and Crawford, G. G. 1966. The use of court probation in the management of the alcohol addict. Am. J. Psychiatry 122:757–762.

Ditman, K. S., Crawford, G. G., Forgy, E. W., Moskowitz, H., and MacAndrew, C. A. 1967. A controlled experiment on the use of court probation for drunk arrests. Am. J. Psychiatry 124:160–163.

Edelman, R. I., and Snead, R. 1972. Self-disclosure in a simulated psychiatric interview. J. Consult. Clin. Psychol. 38:354–358.

Edwards, G. 1972. Diagnosis of schizophrenia: An Anglo-American comparison. Br. J. Psychiatry 120:385–390.

Edwards, G., and Guthrie, S. 1967. A controlled trial of inpatient and outpatient treatment of alcohol dependency. Lancet 555–559.

Ellis, A. 1957. Outcome of employing three techniques of psychotherapy. J. Clin. Psychol. 13:344–350.

Ellis, A. 1962. Reason and Emotion in Psychotherapy. Lyle Stuart, New York.

· Emrick, C. D. 1974. A review of psychologically oriented treatment of alcoholism: I. The use and interrelationship of outcome criteria and drinking behavior following treatment. Quart. J. Stud. Alc. 35:523–549.

Emrick, C. D. 1975. A review of psychologically oriented treatment of alcoholism: II. The relative effectiveness of treatment versus no treatment. J. Stud. Alc. 37:1055–1060.

Emrick, C. D., Lassen, C. L., and Edwards, M. T. 1977. Nonprofessional peers as therapeutic agents. In A. S. Gurman and A. M. Razin (eds.), Effective

Psychotherapy: A Handbook of Research, pp. 120–161. Pergamon Press, New York.

Emrick, C. D., and Stilson, D. W. 1977. The Rand Report: Reworking the Stanford Research Institute Data. J. Stud. Alc. 38:152–163.

Esterly, R. W. 1971. The alcoholic rehabilitation program in the Prince George's County Division of Parole and Probation. Maryland State Med. J. 20:81–84.

Faillace, L. A., Vourlekis, A., and Szara, S. 1970. Hallucinogenic drugs in the treatment of alcoholism: A two year followup. Comprehensive Psychiatry 11:51–56.

Ferguson, F. N. 1970. A treatment program for Navaho alcoholics: Results after four years. Quart. J. Stud. Alc. 31:898–919.

Fiedler, F. E. 1950. A comparison of therapeutic relationship in psychoanalytic, non-directions, and Adlerian therapy. J. Consult. Psychol. 14:436–445.

Final Report—Weighted Caseload Study. October 1976. Prepared for the Administrative Office of the Courts, Commonwealth of Kentucky. Arthur Young & Co., 2707 Citizens Plaza, Louisville, Ky 40202.

Finn, J. D. 1974. A General Model for Multivariate Analysis. Holt, Rinehart & Winston, Inc., New York.

Finney, J. C. 1966. Factor structure with the new set of MMPI Scales and the formula correction. J. Clin. Psychol. 22:443–449.

Finney, J. C. 1973. Automated psychodiagnostic testing for physicians and psychiatrists. In S. K. Bronstein (ed.), Automation and Medicine, pp. 105–121. Futura, Mt. Kisco, New York.

Finney, J. C., Smith, D. F., Skeeters, D. E., and Auvenshine, C. D. 1971. MMPI alcoholism scales: Factor structure and content analysis. Quart. J. Stud. Alc. 32:1055–1060.

Fitzhugh, L. C., Fitzhugh, K. D., and Reitan, R. M. 1960. Adaptive abilities and intellectual functioning in hospitalized alcoholics. Quart. J. Stud. Alc. 21:414–423.

Fitzhugh, L. C., Fitzhugh, K. B., and Reitan, R. M. 1965. Adaptive abilities and intellectual functioning of hospitalized alcoholics: Further consideration. Quart. J. Stud. Alc. 26:402–411.

Forgione, A. G., and Barber, T. X. 1971. A strain guage pain stimulator. Psychophysiology 8:102–106.

Foster, F. M., Horn, J. L., and Wanberg, K. W. 1972. Dimensions of treatment outcome: A factor-analysis study of alcohol responses to a followup questionnaire. Quart. J. Stud. Alc. 33:1079–1098.

Fox, R. 1957. Treatment of alcoholism. In H. E. Himwich (ed.), Alcoholism: Basic Aspects and Treatment, Publication #47. The American Association for the Advancement of Science, Washington, D.C.

Frank, J. D. 1973. Persuasion and Healing. 2nd Ed. Johns Hopkins Press, Baltimore.

Gallant, D. M., Bishop, M. P., Faulkner, M. A., Simpson, L., Cooper, A., Lathrop, D., Brisolara, A. M., and Bossetta, J. R. 1968a. A comparative evaluation of compulsory (group therapy and/or antabuse) and voluntary treatment of the chronic alcoholic municipal court offender. Psychomotus 9:349–352.

Gallant, D. M., Bishop, M. P., Mouledoux, A. M., Faulkner, M. A., Brisoara, A., and Swanson, W. A. 1973. The revolving-door alcoholic. Arch. Gen. Psychiatry 28:633–635.

Gallant, D. M., Faulkner, M., Story, B., ˙Bishop, M. P., Langdon, D. 1968b. Enforced clinic treatment of paroled criminal alcoholics. Quart. J. Stud. Alc. 29:77–83.

Gallant, D. M., Rich, A., Bey, E., and Terraroua, L. 1970. Group psychotherapy with married patients: A successful technique in New Orleans alcoholism clinic patients. J. Louisiana Med. Soc. 122:41–44.

Garfield, S. L., and Bergin, A. E. (eds.). 1978. Handbook of Psychotherapy and Behavior Change: An Empirical Analysis. 2nd Ed. John Wiley & Sons, Inc., New York.

Gellman, I. P. 1964. The Sober Alcoholic: An Organizational Analysis of Alcoholics Anonymous. College of University Press, New Haven, Conn.

Gerard, D. L., and Saenger, G. 1966. Outpatient Treatment of Alcoholism: A Study of Outcome and its Determinants. University of Toronto Press, Toronto.

Goldfried, M. R. 1969. Prediction of improvement in an alcoholism outpatient clinic. Quart. J. Stud. Alc. 30:129–139.

Goodman, D. (In collaboration with Maultsby, M.) 1974. Emotional Well-being through Rational Behavior Training. Charles C Thomas Publisher, Springfield.

Gray, W. S. 1955. Standardized Oral Reading Paragraphs, pp. 1–4. Bobbs-Merrill Co., Inc., Indianapolis.

Guerney, B. G. 1969. Psychotherapeutic Agents: New Roles for Nonprofessionals, Parents, and Teachers. Holt, Rinehart & Winston, Inc., New York.

Gurman, A. S., and Razin, A. M. (eds.). 1977. Effective Psychotherapy: A Handbook of Research. Pergamon Press, New York.

Haberman, P. W., and Scheinberg, J. M. 1969. Public attitudes toward alcoholism as an illness. Am. J. Pub. Health 59:1209–1216.

Halstead, W. G., and Wepman, J. M. 1949. The Halstead-Wepman aphasia screening test. J. Speech Hear. Disord. 14:9–15.

Harris, J. B. 1975. An abbreviated form of the Phillips Rating Scale of Premorbid Adjustment in Schizophrenia. J. Abnorm. Psychol. 84:124–137.

Hathaway, S. R., and McKinley, J. C. 1943. Minnesota Multiphasic Personality Inventory. Psychological Corporation, New York.

Hayman, M. 1956. Current attitudes to alcoholism of psychiatrists in southern California. Am. J. Psychiatry 112:484–493.

Heimburger, R. D., and Reitan, R. M. 1961. Easily administered written test for lateralizing brain lesions. J. Neurosurg. 18:301–312.

Hill, M., and Blane, H. T. 1967. Evaluation of psychotherapy with alcoholics. Quart. J. Stud. Alc. 78:76–104.

Hoffer, A. 1967. A program for the treatment of alcoholism: LSD, malvaria and nicotinic acid. In H. A. Abramson (ed.), The Use of LSD in Psychotherapy and Alcoholism, pp. 343–406. Bobbs-Merrill Co., Inc., New York.

Hollingshead, A. B. 1957. Two-factor index of Social Position. Unpublished manuscript. (Available from author: 1965 Yale Station, New Haven, Conn.)

Horn, J. L., and Wanberg, K. W. 1969. Symptom patterns related to excessive use of alcohol. Quart. J. Stud. Alc. 30:35–58.

Hornstra, L. K., Lubin, B., Lewis, R., and Willis, B. 1972. Worlds apart, patients and professionals. Arch. Gen. Psychiatry 27:553–557.

Jellinek, E. M. 1960. The Disease Concept of Alcoholism. Hillhouse, Highland Park, N.J.

Jellinek, E. M., Isbell, H., Lundquist, G., Tiebait, H. M., Duchene, H., Mardones, J., and MacLeod, L. D. 1955. The craving for alcohol: A symposium. Quart. J. Stud. Alc. 16:34–66.

Jindra, N. J., and Forslund, M. A. 1978. AA in a western city. J. Stud. Alc. 39:111–120.

Karlsruher, A. E. 1974. The nonprofessional as a psychotherapeutic agent: A review of the empirical evidence pertaining to his effectiveness. Am. J. Commun. Psychol. 2:61–77.

Keller, M. 1976. The disease concept of alcoholism revisited. J. Stud. Alc. 37:1694–1715.

Kent, G. H. 1946. Manual: Series of Emergency Scales, pp. 1–8. Psychological Corporation, New York.

Khoury, N. J., and Pearson, A. W. 1961. Alcoholism: Medical team approach to treatment. California Med. 95:284–287.

Kimmel, M. E. 1971. Antabuse in a clinic program. Am. J. Nurs. 71:1173–1175.

Kissin, B., Platz, A., and Su, W. H. 1970. Social and psychosocial factors in the treatment of chronic alcoholism. J. Psychiatric Res. 8:13–27.

Kissin, B., Rosenblatt, S. M., and Machover, S. 1968. Prognostic factors in alcoholism. Psychiatric Res. Rep. 64:22–43.

Klanknecht, R. A., and Goldstein, S. G. 1972. Neuropsychological defects associated with alcoholism: A review and discussion. Quart. J. Stud. Alc. 33:999–1019.

Kurland, A. A. 1968. Maryland alcoholics: Followup study. Psychiatric Res. Rep. 24:71–82.

Lal, S. 1969. Metronidazole in the treatment of alcoholism: A clinical trial and review of the literature. Quart. J. Stud. Alc. 30:140–151.

Leach, B., Norris, J. L., Dancey, T., and Biassell, L. 1969. Dimensions in Alcoholics Anonymous: 1935–1965. Int. J. Addict. 4(4):507–541.

Luborsky, L., Singer, B., and Luborsky, L. 1975. Comparative studies of psychotherapies. Arch. Gen. Psychiatry 32:995–1008.

Ludwig, A. M., Levine, J., and Stark, L. H. 1970. LSD and Alcoholism: A clinical Study of Treatment Efficacy. Charles C Thomas Publisher, Springfield.

Ludwig, A. M., and Stark, L. H. 1974. Alcohol craving: Subjective and situational aspects. Quart. J. Stud. Alc. 35:108–130.

Ludwig, A. M., and Wikler, A. 1974. Craving and relapse to drink. Quart. J. Stud. Alc. 35:108–130.

Ludwig, A. M., Wikler, A., and Stark, L. H. 1974. The first drink. Arch. Gen. Psychiatry 30:539–547.

Maier, R. A., and Fox, V. 1958. Forced therapy of probated alcoholics. Med. Times. 86:1051–1054.

Marlatt, G. A., and Gordon, J. R. 1979. Determinants of relapse: Implications for the maintainance of behavior change. In P. Davidson (ed.), Behavioral Medicine: Changing Health Lifestyles. Brunner/Mazel, New York.

Maultsby, M. C. 1971a. Handbook of Rational Self-Counseling. The Association for Rational Thinking, Madison, Wisc.

Maultsby, M. C. 1971b. Systematic written homework in psychotherapy. Psychother.: Theory. Res. Pract. 8:195–198.

Maultsby, M. C. 1975. Help Yourself to Happiness through Rational Self-Counseling. Herman Publishing, Inc., Boston.

Maultsby, M. C. 1979. A Million Dollars for your Hangover. Rational Self Help Books, Lexington, Ky.

Mayer, J., and Myerson, D. J. 1965. Outpatient treatment of alocholics: Effects of status, stability and nature of treatment. Quart. J. Stud. Alc. 26:480–485.

Mello, N. K. 1972. Behavioral studies of alcoholism. In B. Kissin and H. Begleiter, The Biology of Alcoholism. Plenum Press, New York.

Meltzoff, H., and Kornreich, M. 1970. Research in Psychotherapy. Atherton, New York.

Mendelson, J., and Chafetz, M. 1959. Alcoholism is an emergency ward problem. Quart. J. Stud. Alc. 20:270–275.

Mensh, N. 1953. Kent series of emergency scales. In O. K. Buros (ed.), The Fourth

Mental Measurements Yearbook, pp. 347–348. Rutgers University Press, New Brunswick, N.J.

Miller, W. R. 1976. Alcoholism scales and objective assessment methods: A review. Psychol. Bull. 83(4):649–674.

Mindlin, D. F. 1959. The characteristics of alcoholics as related to prediction of therapeutic outcome. Quart. J. Stud. Alc. 20:604–619.

Mindlin, D. F. 1960. Evaluation of therapy for alcoholics in a workhouse setting. Quart. J. Stud. Alc. 21:90–112.

Mooney, R. L., and Gordon, L. V. 1950. The Mooney Problem Check Lists Manual. The Psychological Corporation, New York.

Moore, R. A., and Ramseur, F. 1960. Effects of psychotherapy in an open-ward hospital in-patients with alcoholism. Quart. J. Stud. Alc. 21:233–252.

Myerson, D. J., Mackay, J., Wallens, A., and Neiberg, N. 1961. A report of a rehabilitation program for alcoholic women prisoners. Quart. J. Stud. Alc. Suppl. 1:151–157.

Nash, E., Frank, J., and Gildeman, L. 1957. Some factors related to patients remaining in group psychotherapy. Int. J. Group Psychother. 7:264–274.

Nathan, P. E., and Harris, S. L. 1975. Mental status exam. Psychopathology and Society, pp. 122–123. McGraw-Hill Book Co., New York.

National Council on Alcoholism, Criteria Committee. 1972. Criteria for the diagnosis of alcoholism. Ann. Intern. Med. 77:249–258.

NIAAA. 1974. First Special Report to Congress on Alcohol and Health. Bethesda, Maryland.

NIAAA. 1978. Third Special Report to Congress on Alcohol and Health. Bethesda, Maryland.

Norvig, J., and Nielson, B. 1956. A follow-up study of 221 alcohol addicts in Denmark. Quart. J. Stud. Alc. 17:633–642.

Page, R. D., and Linden, F. D. 1974. Reversible organic brain syndrome in alcoholics: A psychometric evaluation. Quart. J. Stud. Alc. 35:98–107.

Pattison, E. M., Sobell, M. B., and Sobell, L. C. 1977. Emerging Concepts of Alcohol Dependence. Springer Publishing Co., New York.

Perrett, L. F. 1972. Immediate and background contextual effects in clinical judgement. Dissert. Abstr. Int. 32:4224.

Petrie, A. 1967. Individuality in Pain and Suffering. The University of Chicago Press, Chicago.

Pittman, D. J., and Tate, R. L. 1969. A comparison of two treatment programs for alcoholics. Quart. J. Stud. Alc 30:888–899.

Pokorny, A. D., Miller, B. A., and Cleveland, S. E. 1968. Response to treatment of alcoholism: A follow-up study. Quart. J. Stud. Alc. 29:364–381.

Prothro, W. D. 1961. Alcoholics can be rehabilitated. Am. J. Pub. Health 51:450–461.

Prothro, W. D. 1963. Inpatient versus outpatient alcoholism rehabilitation. J. Michigan State Med. Soc. 62:1004–1007.

Redlich, F. C., and Freedman, D. X. 1966. The Theory and Practice of Psychiatry. Basic Books, Inc., New York.

Reitan, R. M. 1955. The relation of the Trail Making Test to organic brain damage. J. Consult. Psychol. 19:393–449.

Reitan, R. M. 1958a. Trail Making Test. Manual for Administration, Scoring and Administration. Unpublished manuscript. (Available from author: 708 89th Place S.E., Mercer Island, Washington 98040.)

Reitan, R. M. 1958b. The validity of the Trail Making Test as an indicator of organic brain damage. Percept. Motor Skills 8:271–276.

Reitan, R. M. 1962. Psychological deficit. Ann. Rev. Psychol. 13:415–444.

Reitan, R. M., and Davison, L. A. (eds.). 1974. Clinical Neuropsychology: Current Status and Applications. John Wiley & Sons, Inc., New York.

Reitan, R. M., and Tarshes, E. L. 1959. Differential effects of lateralized brain lesions on the Trail Making Test. J. Nerv. Ment. Dis. 129:257–262.

Ringer, C., Kufner, H., Antons, K., and Feuerlein, W. 1977. The N.C.A. criteria for the diagnosis of alcoholism. J. Stud. Alc. 38:1259–1273.

Ritson, E. D. 1968. The prognosis of alcohol addicts treated by a specialist unit. Br. J. Psychiatry 144:1019–1029.

Robson, R. A., Paulus, I., and Clarke, G. G. 1965. An evaluation of the effect of a clinical treatment program on the rehabilitation of alcoholic patients. Quart. J. Stud. Alc. 26:264–278.

Rohan, W. P. 1970. A follow-up study of hospitalized problem drinkers. Dis. Nerv. Syst. 31:259–267.

Root, L. 1973. In-service training of the para-professional in the field of alcoholism. In G. Staub and L. Kent (eds.), The Para-professional in the Treatment of Alcoholism. Charles C Thomas Publisher, Springfield.

Rosenberg, C., Gerrin, J., Manohar, V., and Liftik, H. 1976. Evaluation of training of alcoholism counselors. J. Stud. Alc. 37:1236–1246.

Routh, D. K., and King, K. M. 1972. Social class bias in clinical judgment. J. Consult. Clin. Psychol. 38:202–207.

Russell, P., and Brandsma, J. M. 1974. A theoretical and empirical integration of the rational-emotions and classical conditioning theories. J. Consult. Clin. Psychol. 42(3):389–397.

Sandifer, M. G. 1972. Science and set in treatment decisions. Am. J. Psychiatry 128:1140–1145.

Shaw, S., Cartwright, A., Spratley, T., and Harwin, J. 1978. Responding to Drinking Problems. University Park Press, Baltimore.

Sheuerman, A., Pearman, E., and Glass, L. 1961. A study of 54 compulsory referrals to a community alcoholic rehabilitation clinic. California Alc. Rev. 4:13–15.

Sloane, R. B., Staples, F. R., Cristol, A. H., Yorkston, N.J., and Whipple, K. 1975. Psychotherapy versus Behavior Therapy. Harvard University Press, Cambridge.

Smart, R. G., Storm, T., Baker, E. F. W., and Solursk, L. 1966. A controlled study of lysergide in the treatment of alcoholism. I. The effects on drinking behavior. Quart. J. Stud. Alc. 27:469–482.

Smart, R. G., Storm, T., Baker, E. F. W., and Solursk, L. A. 1967. LSD in the treatment of alcoholism; an investigation of its effects on drinking behavior, personality structure, and social functioning. Brookside Monograph No. 6. University of Toronto Press, Toronto.

Sobell, M. B., Sobell, L. C., and Samuels, F. H. 1974. Validity of self reports of alcohol-related arrests by alcoholics. Quart. J. Stud. Alc. 35:276–280.

Staub, G., and Kent, L. 1973. The Para-professional in the Treatment of Alcoholism. Charles C Thomas Publisher, Springfield.

Stein, L. I., Newton, J. R. and Bowman, R. S. 1975. Duration of hospitalization for alcoholics. Archives of General Psychiatry 32:247–252.

Stein, L. I., Niles, D., and Ludwig, A. M. 1968. Loss of control phenomenon in alcoholics. Quart. J. Stud. Alc. 29:598–602.

Ullman, L. P., and Krasner, L. 1970. A Psychological Approach to Abnormal Behavior. Holt, Rinehart & Winston, Inc., New York.

Viamontes, J. A. 1972. Review of drug effectiveness in the treatment of alcoholism. Am. J. Psychiatry 128:1570–1571.

Welsh, G. S. 1952. A factor study of the MMPI using scales with item overlap limited. Am. Psychol. 7:341.

Willems, T. J., Letemendia, F. J., and Arroyable, F. 1973. A two-year followup study comparing short- with long-term inpatient treatment of alcholics. Br. J. Psychiatry 122:637–648.

Wolberg, L. R. 1967. The Technique of Psychotherapy. Grune & Stratton, New York.

Wright, H. F., MacPhee, H. M., and Cummings, S. D. 1949. The relationship between the Kent EGY and the Bellevue Verbal Scale. J. Abnorm. Soc. Psychol. 44:233–245.

Yapalater, A. R. 1965. Rehabilitation program for alcoholic inmates at the Westchester County Penitentiary. New York State J. Med. 65:1003–1011.

Zax, M., and Cowen, E. 1976. Abnormal Psychology: Changing Conceptions: Holt, Rinehart & Winston, New York.

Zax, M. R., Marsey, R., and Biggs, C. F. 1961. Demographic characteristics of alcoholic outpatients and the tendency to remain in treatment. Quart. J. Stud. Alc. 22:98–105.

Index

AA, *see* Alcoholics Anonymous
Al-Anon, *see* Alcoholics Anonymous
Alcohol
  abstinence from, 53, 55, 85, 104
  physiological reactions to overcon-
    sumption of, 1
Alcohol vs. money, 70
Alcoholic, 81, 88, 95, 103, 106, 107,
  114
  arrests of, cost of, 101-102
  classification of, 25
  dropout rate for, 89
  dynamics of personality of, 25
  primary (essential), 25
  referral of, 15
  "revolving door," 63, 95, 117
  secondary (symptomatic), 25
  subjects determined as, 40-41, 64
  treatment of, conclusions regarding,
    117-118
  treatment programs for, problems
    with present day, 86-87
  see also Subject(s)
Alcoholics Anonymous, 1, 2, 7, 44, 85,
  100
  assignment to, 34
  follow-up on, results of 3-month,
    105
  follow-up on results of 12-month,
    105
  at intake, results of, 103
  interaction on Hysteria Scale, 79, 116
  methodology of, 17, 33-34
  at outcome, results of, 104
  in practice, 34
  profile of members of, 11-12
  program
    alternatives to, 114
    limitations of, 84
  review of literature on, 12
  theory of, 33-34
  see also Self-help methods
Alcoholism, 53, 86
  conceptual models and treatments of,
    13
  criteria used in constructing Drinking
    Questionnaire, 134-135
  diagnosis of, 40-41
  as disease, 1, 85, 86
  incidence of, 1
  prevalence of, 1, 85
  review of the literature concerning,
    7-13
  as symptom, 1-2, 24-25, 85, 86
ANOVA, *see* One-way analysis of
  variance
Arrest records, 70-101
  of AA group, analysis of, 104
  analysis of, 64, 65, 98-99, 104, 113
  of coerced subjects, analysis of,
    98-99
  of lay-RBT group, analysis of, 104,
    113
  used as outcome measures, 56-58
  of voluntary subjects, analysis of,
    98-99

Behavioral measures, 115
  alcohol offered by experimenter, 47
  working for money and alcohol, 46,
    90
  see also Follow-up; Predictor
    paradigm
Behavior Rating Scale, 59, 70, 74, 89,
  100, 108, 116, 158-167,
  170-174
  comparison with BRS-R, 82
  follow-up, analysis of results of,
    75-77
  instrumentation of, 53-55
  repeated measures analyses of, 77-78
  see also Follow-up; Outcome
    measures
Breathalizer
  instrumentation of, 46
  results of, 82
  see also Follow-up; Instrumentation
BRS, *see* Behavior Rating Scale

Chi square, 61, 70, 73, 74, 75, 89, 96,
  97, 103, 109
Clients
  analyses, number of subjects in, 97

Clients — *continued*
  by the court system, 95
  the efficacy of, 34, 95–102, 116–117
  in Self-Help Alcoholism Research
    Project, methodology of,
    95–96
  see also subjects
Control group, 13, 77, 81, 99, 108
  arrest records of, 99, 104
  assignment to, 34–35
  attendance of subjects in, 98
  improvement rate of, 74, 110
  at intake, 70, 90, 96, 109
  at 3-month follow-up, 83, 92, 105,
    112
  at 12-month follow-up, 92, 105, 112
  at outcome, 72, 90–92, 96, 97, 104,
    110–112
  "new" system
    arrest records of subjects referred
      by, 98–99
    attendance of subjects referred by,
      98
    defined, 95–96
    dropout rate of subjects referred
      by, 96–97
  "old" system
    arrest records of subjects referred
      by, 98–99
    attendance of subjects referred by,
      98
    defined, 95–96
    dropout rate of subjects referred
      by, 96–97
  referral form, 124
Craving, 47
  defined, 32
  in relation to loss of control, 51–52
  in relation to pain tolerance, 46
Craving and Withdrawal Questionnaire,
    70, 77, 152–155
  as change measure, 51
  instrumentation of, 51–52
  as predictor of treatment outcome,
    51

Demographics, 48–51, 70, 109, 115,
    142–147
Drawing Test, instrumentation of,
    41–42
Drinking indices, 174–184

  analysis of, 63, 91, 104–105, 109–112,
    115
  computation of drinking/occasion
    proportion, 180–181
  drinks/day proportion in, 183
  frequency of consumption (for
    Volume-Variability Index),
    182
  instrumentation of, 55
  Quantity-Frequency-Variability Clas-
    sifications, 179
  Quantity-Frequency-Variability scales
    for, computation of ethanol
    intake from, 176
  Quantity-Frequency-Volume Index,
    55
  Quantity-Variability classifications of
    Q-F-V Index, 177–178
  Quantity-Volume Index, 55
  used as outcome measures, 55
  Volume-Pattern Index, 55
  Volume-Variability Index, 55, 184
Drinking Questionnaire, 130–132
  analysis of responses to, by dropouts
    and completors, 196–198
  analysis of results of, 64, 65, 68–69,
    109–112
  instrumentation of, 40–41
Dropout rate
  for alcoholics, 89
  for Self-Help Alcoholism Research
    Project, 96–97, 109
  for self-help programs, 104
  for various programs, 89
Dropouts, 32, 35, 36, 71, 96, 115
  analysis of, 68–69, 83
  for all accepted clients, percentage
    of, 97
  for coerced subjects, percentage of,
    97
  compared with completors on
    screening and drinking ques-
    tionnaires, 196–198
  defined for SHARP program, 89
  the problem of, 9–10
  for voluntary subjects, percentage of,
    97
Dropping out, reasons for, 98

Finger Pain Tolerance Test, 70, 77

instrumentation of, 44–46
results of, 82
Finney Addiction Scale, 80, 116
Follow-up, 83, 84, 89, 99, 113, 114, 117
on AA group, results of, 77
BRS
  analysis of results of, 75–77
  results of repeated measures analyses of, 77–78
  instrumentation of behavioral measures at, 46–47
  alcohol offered by experimenter, 47
  working for money and alcohol, 46
instrumentation of Behavior Rating Scale at, 53–54, 116
instrumentation of Breathalizer Test at, 46
instrumentation of Craving and Withdrawal Questionnaire at, 51
instrumentation of predictor paradigm at, 52
MMPI
  analysis of results of, 74–75
  results of repeated measures analyses of, 78–82
results of, 74–77
3-month
  comparison of self-help and control groups at, 105, 106
  comparison of therapy and control groups at, 92, 112
  results of, 92, 105, 112
12-month
  comparison of self-help and control groups at, 105, 106
  comparison of therapy and control groups at, 92, 112
  results of, 92, 105, 112–113
see also Outcome measures
Forms
  authorization, for voluntary clients, 122
  Behavior Rating Scale and scoring key—drinking, 170–174
  Behavior Rating Scale and scoring keys—social, employment, economic, and legal, 158–167
  contract, legal, 126
  Craving and Withdrawal Questionnaire, 152–155

demographic questionnaire, 142–147
  Drinking Questionnaire and scoring key, 130–132
  evaluation, therapist, 186–188
  Mental Status Interview, 128
  problem checklist, 150
  referral, court, 124

Hypochondriasis Scale, 79, 116
Hysteria Scale, 79, 116

Indicators
  of age, 67
  of alcoholism, 65
  of brain functioning, 66
  of intellectual functioning, 66
  of legal difficulties, 65, 113
  of socioeconomic status, 67
Inpatient treatment, 9, 51, 54, 85, 90, 108
  compulsory, 95
  see also Therapy; Treatment
Insight, in therapy, 24
Insight therapy, 87, 88
  at intake, results of, 90
  interaction on Hypochondriasis Scale, 79, 116
  interaction on Hysteria Scale, 79, 116
  methodology of, 15–16, 23–27
  at outcome, results of, 83, 90–92
  in practice, 26–27
  theory of, 23–26
  therapists for, 87, 88
  at 3-month follow-up, results of, 92
  at 12-month follow-up, results of, 92
  see also Therapy; Treatment
Instrumentation
  of behavioral measures, 46–47
  of Behavior Rating Scale, 53–55
  of Breathalizer Test, 46
  of Craving and Withdrawal Questionnaire, 51–52
  of demographic questions, 47–51
  of Drawing Test, 41–42
  of drinking indices, 55
  of Drinking Questionnaire, 40–41
  of Finger Pain Tolerance Test, 44–46
  of Intelligence Test, 40
  of Mental Status Interview, 39

Instrumentation — *continued*
    of Minnesota Multiphasic Personality
        Inventory, 52–53
    of outcome measures, 52–59
    of predictor paradigm, 52
    of problem checklist, 51
    of Reading Test, 43–44
    of screening procedures, 39–46
    of self-report measures, 47–52
    of therapist evaluation form, 58–59
    of Trail Making Test, 42–43
    statistics of self-help and control
        groups at, 103
    statisics of therapy and control
        groups at, 90, 108
Intelligence Test
    analysis of results of, 64–65, 66, 68
    instrumentation of, 40
Interview, measures employed at each
    testing, 70

Kent IQ (Kent Scale measured intelli-
    gence), *see* Intelligence Test

Mann-Whitney U Test, 70, 71, 72
Mental Status Interview, 128
    of Alcoholics Anonymous, 17
    analysis of, 61
    of assignment to programs, 22
    of coercion in Self-Help Alcoholism
        Research Project, 95–96
    of control group, 23
    of criteria for evaluation of outcome
        research, 36–37
    of criteria for inclusion in treatment
        sample, 35–36
    of experimental groups, 23–34
    of insight therapy, 15–16
    instrumentation of, 39
    of payment, 17
    of rational behavior therapy (non-
        professional), 16–17
    of rational behavior therapy (pro-
        fessoinal), 16
    of screening procedures, 20–23
    of termination procedures, 35
    of treatments, 23–34
Minnesota Multiphasic Personality
    Inventory (MMPI)

comparisons of main effects for the
    time variable, 82
follow-up, analysis of results of,
    74–75, 83–84
instrumentation of, 52–53
used as outcome measure, 52–53
MMPI, *see* Minnesota Multiphasic
    Personality Inventory

Need, defined, 31–32

One-way analysis of variance
    (ANOVA), 70, 72, 74, 75, 89,
    98, 103, 108
    time-repeated measures of, 110
Outcome
    battery, 17
    pain tolerance as predictor of treat-
        ment, 46
    research, evaluation of, 36–37
    results at, 115–116
    statistics of self-help and control
        groups at, 104–105
    statistics of therapy and control
        groups at, 90–91, 109–112
Outcome measures
    AA group membership in relation to,
        73
    analysis of, 69–74, 90–91
    arrest records used as, 56–58
    Behavior Rating Scale, 53–55
    drinking indices, 55
    instrumentation of, 52–59
    Minnesota Multiphasic Personality
        Inventory, 52–53
Outpatient treatment, 9, 51, 86, 88, 108
    as alternative to hospital, 86–87
    compulsory, 95
    problems of, 87
    see also Therapy; Treatment

Personality
    "hysterical type," 25
    "phallic-Oedipal type," 25
    in relation to pain tolerance, 46
    types relative to alcoholism, 25
Predictor
    Craving and Withdrawal Question-
        naire used as, 51–52

Finger Pain Tolerance Test used as, 46
paradigm, 52
working for money and alcohol used as, 46
Predictor analyses, 82

Rational behavior therapy, 44, 107
Rational behavior therapy (nonprofessional)
follow-up on
results of 3-month, 105
results of 12-month, 105
intake, results at, 103
methodology of, 16-17, 32-33
outcome, results at, 104, 115
in practice, 32-33
see also Self-help methods
Rational behavior therapy (professional)
follow-up on
results of 3-month, 92
results of 12-month, 92
intake, results at, 90
methodology, 16, 27-32
outcome, results at, 90-91
in practice, 30-32
therapists for, 87, 88
theory of, 27-30
RBT, *see* Rational behavior therapy
Reading Test
analysis of results of, 64-65
instrumentation of, 43-44
Oral, direction and rationale for scoring of modified Gray, 138-139

Screening procedures
analysis of, 61-63
Drawing Test, 41-42
Drinking Questionnaire, 40-41, 130-132
dropouts vs. completors, 196-198
instrumentation of, 39-46
Intelligence Test, 40
Mental Status Interview, 39, 128
methodology of, 20-23
Reading Test, 43-44
Reading Test, direction and rationale for scoring, 138-139

results of, 61
statistical tables for accepted vs. rejected clients, 190-193
Trail Making Test (TMT), 42-43
Self-Help Alcoholism Research Project, 5, 15, 36, 55, 87
AA program of, 17
conclusions drawn from, 115-118
patient flow chart of, 18-19
programs, retention rate of, 89
purpose of, 2, 115
referral of subjects to, 3, 4, 20, 21-22
therapists, employed by, 88
Self-help methods
follow-up of
3-month, 105, 106
12-month, 105, 106
intake results of, analysis of, 103
outcome results of, analysis of, 104-105
results of, 103-106
see also Alcoholics Anonymous; Rational behavior therapy (nonprofessional)
Self-report measures
Craving and Withdrawal Questionnaire, 51-52, 152-155
demographic characteristics questionnaire, 47-51, 142-147
problem checklist, 51, 150
SHARP, *see* Self-Help Alcoholism Research Project
Student Neuman-Keuls Procedure, paired comparisons employing, 89, 96, 109, 111, 112
Subjects
accepted into SHARP, 61
profile of, 115
coerced
analysis of arrest records of, 98-99
analysis of BRS for, 100
attendance records of, 97-98
dropout rate of, 96-97
comparison of accepted vs. rejected, 62, 190-193
profile of, 63
screening of, 20-23, 39-44, 61
of SHARP, changes in, 116
of treatment sample, analysis of, 63-66

Subjects — *continued*
  voluntary, 96, 97, 98
    analysis of arrest records of,
      98–99
    analysis of BRS for, 100
    attendance records of, 97–98
    authorization form for, 122
    dropout rate of, 96–97

Therapist
  evaluation form, instrumentation of,
    58–59
  evaluation of subjects, analysis of re-
    sults of, 74
  evaluation of subjects by, 70
  imported
    defined, 87
    virtues of program, 92–93
  nonprofessional, 107, 108, 110
  nonprofessional, advantages of the,
    107–108, 109
  professional, 107, 108, 110
  for pro-RBT and insight therapy pro-
    grams, 87, 88
  working with alcoholics, 86, 87
Therapy
  AA
    interaction on Finney Addiction
      Scale, 80, 81
    interaction on Hysteria Scale, 79,
      81
    results of, 72, 73, 83
  analysis of results of, 89–92
  behavioral, 8–9, 12
  client-centered, 8
  comparison of pro-RBT and insight
    groups at 3-month follow-up,
    92
  comparison of pro-RBT and insight
    groups at 12-month follow-up,
    92
  conclusions regarding comparison of,
    9, 12
  criticism of psychotherapy, 15
  group, 8, 27, 32–33, 89
  individual, 8, 27, 32–33
  insight, 2, 12, 15–16, 83
    interaction on Hypochondriasis
      Scale, 80
    interaction on Hysteria Scale, 79,
      81

    results of, 71 72, 73
    results of, compared with pro-RBT
      and control groups, 90–93
  layman-administered
    results of, at intake, 109, 111
    results of, at outcome, 109–112
    results of, at 3-month follow-up,
      112
    results of, at 12-month follow-up,
      112
  lay-RBT, 83
    interaction on Finney Addiction
      Scale, 80, 81, 116
    interaction on Hypochondriasis
      Scale, 80, 116
    interaction on Hysteria Scale, 79,
      81, 116
    results of, 71, 72, 73, 77, 78
  professionally administered
    compared with layman-adminis-
      tered, 107, 114
    results of, at intake, 109, 111
    results of, at outcome, 109–112
    results of, at 3-month follow-up,
      112
    results of, at 12-month follow-up,
      112
  pro-RBT, 83
    interaction on Finney Addiction
      Scale, 80, 81, 116
    interaction on Hypochondriasis
      Scale, 80, 116
    results of, 72, 73, 79
    results of, compared with insight
      and control groups, 90–93
  psychological, 7–8
  rational behavior, 16
  rational-emotive, 8, 27
  time-limited, 8
  see also Alcoholics Anonymous; Al-
    cholism; Insight therapy;
    Rational behavior therapy;
    Self-Help Alcoholism
    Research Project; Treatment
TMT, *see* Trail Making Test
Trail Making Test, 41, 68
  analysis of results of, 64–65, 66
  instrumentation of, 42–43
  of alcoholics, conclusions regard-
    ing, 117–118
Treatment
  comparison of different schools of, 8

compulsory, 11, 34, 73, 84, 105–106
compulsory, compared with volun-
        tary, 95, 105–106
days in/number of sessions of,
        70–71, 83, 98, 104, 109
follow-up, 11, 15, 17
groups, improvement rate of, 74
hospital, problems of, 86, 87
inpatient, 9, 51, 54
outpatient, 9, 15, 51
    problems of, 87
programs
    analysis of assignment to, 66–68
    assignment to, 13, 22, 109
    outcome of various, 48, 49,
        113–114
    success in alcohol, 47, 48, 105,
        111, 113–114
    see also Alcoholics Anonymous;
        Alcoholism; Insight Therapy;
        Rational behavior therapy;
        Self-Help Alcoholism Re-
        search Project; Therapy
Treatment modalities, 2, 15, 87
    differentiable, determination of, 69
t statistic, 61

Variables
    analysis of, 70, 108–109
    of behavior, 47–52
    client
        as predictors of client improve-
            ment, 50
        in relation to treatment outcome,
            48, 50
    dependent
        analysis of results concerning, 71,
            109

repeated measures analyses of,
        77–82
derived from MMPI, repeated
        measures analyses of, 78–82,
        108
drinking, analysis of results concern-
        ing, 73–74, 83, 91, 100,
        104–105, 109–111
drinking (self-report), analysis of
        results concerning social,
        72–73, 111
economic
    analysis of, 71, 83
    at outcome, 90
    at follow-up, 74–77, 92, 105–106,
        112–113
    at intake, 70, 90, 103, 108, 109, 111
    legal (police records), analysis of re-
        sults concerning, 72, 83, 90,
        100, 104, 112
    at outcome, 70, 74, 90–91, 104,
        109–112
    of outcome measures, analysis of,
        69–74, 90–91, 109–112
    "percent treatments attended," 97
    program, in relation to treatment
        outcome, 48, 49
    repeated measures analyses of, 78–82
    treatment holding power, 104
Voluntary (self-referred) subjects, see
        Subjects

Want, defined, 31
Working for money and alcohol
    as change measure, 46
    as predictor of outcome, 46
    see also Behavioral measures, Predic-
        tor paradigm

5